LEGAL STRATEGIES FOR EVERYONE

THE COMPLETE GUIDE TO COVERING YOUR ASSETS, MAXIMIZING WEALTH, AND PROTECTING YOUR FAMILY

MAURICIO J. RAULD, ESQ.

Sam—
    Thanks for being an avid
Drunk Real Estate listener.
We appreciate you.
    Remember, its _YOUR_ way.
                Mauricio

MAURICIO J. RAULD, ESQ.   Vol. 2

LEGAL
STRATEGIES
FOR
EVERYONE

THE COMPLETE GUIDE TO COVERING
YOUR ASSETS, MAXIMIZING WEALTH,
AND PROTECTING YOUR FAMILY

PRESS

Phoenix, Arizona

Published by KM Press

 KM Press
15170 N. Hayden Road
Scottsdale, AZ 85260
480-998-5400

Learn more at: www.kenmcelroy.com

ISBN: 979-8-9895781-2-2 (Print)
ISBN: 979-8-9895781-3-9 (E-Readers)

Printed in the United States of America

RICH FETTKE

The Wise Investor
A Modern Parable About Creating Financial Freedom and Living Your Best Life

MIKE MALONEY

Guide to Investing in Gold & Silver
Protect Your Financial Future

NEW AND COMING SOON FROM KM PRESS

STRATEGIES SERIES

Branding and Marketing Strategies for Everyone

Real Estate Strategies for Everyone

Legal Strategies for Everyone

Sales Strategies for Everyone

Tax Strategies for Everyone

ABCs of Raising Capital
Only Lazy People Use Their Own Money

Speak and Get What You Want
Communicate Like the World's Most Successful Leaders

DEDICATION

To Heidi, Adelina, and Alessandra,
you are my everything.

TABLE OF CONTENTS

INTRODUCTION

Yes, I'm a lawyer.

But don't hold that against me. I'm not your typical lawyer. In fact, I'm affectionately known as "one of the few lawyers who actually speaks English." My superpower is the ability to take complex legal matters and make them easy to understand.

When I was growing up, I never thought about becoming a lawyer. I certainly never envisioned writing a book about legal strategies for everyone. After all, my specialties lie primarily in helping clients raise money from other people and helping people protect their hard-earned assets. You'll notice quite a few strategies in this book on those two themes.

After becoming Ken McElroy's legal adviser a few years back, I started contributing broader legal content to his community at KenMcElroy.com and on his YouTube channel. What I've learned over the years is that the legal strategies I outline in this book aren't merely for corporate entities, millionaires, or those caught up in litigation. They're essential tools for everyone, from the young adult stepping into the workforce to the older individual considering retirement.

My hope in writing this book is to empower you by offering a comprehensive overview of fundamental legal measures that everyone should be aware of. Even if you're at a point in your life where you don't think you need to implement some of these strategies, you'll at least become aware of—and hopefully remember—them when you need them. This book, therefore, doesn't need to be read cover to cover in the order I've presented it. I encourage you to browse the chapters and focus on areas that match your current journey and to use this book as a reference guide, returning to it periodically.

Sprinkled throughout the book are four types of tip boxes:

DEFINITION
legal explanations you may not be aware of

PRO TIP
smart ideas to protect your assets

STRATEGY
simple, mini-tactics within the larger strategy covered in the chapter

WARNING
potential pitfalls to avoid

The book contains ten chapters. Chapter 1 starts by laying the foundation for the concept of asset protection, what it is, and why it's so important. Asset protection strategies are some of the most important strategies I can think of, so several chapters are devoted to different techniques and strategies that involve protecting your hard-earned wealth.

Chapter 2 covers the most fundamental of all asset protection strategies—"own nothing, control everything"—a phrase coined by one of the wealthiest people to ever walk the planet, John D. Rockefeller. The chapter discusses using entities to own your assets and remove ownership so they're kept protected and out of the reach of creditors.

Chapter 3 delves into the delicate subject of your premature death and making sure the government doesn't get to decide who looks after your children if you die unexpectedly. This is not a subject that most of us are comfortable discussing, but it's a critical subject that protects your loved ones—especially your children.

Chapter 4 moves into some money-saving strategies when it comes to dealing with lawyers. So many people unnecessarily waste money on lawyers that I thought I'd dedicate an entire chapter to some strategies for saving a little cash when dealing with my colleagues.

Chapter 5 then pivots to a topic that many consider me to be the foremost expert on: creative strategies for raising money from other people to acquire real estate, businesses, and investments—or leveraging the power of other people's money.

With this ever-changing world of digital assets, such as social media accounts, e-mail, photos, cryptocurrencies, NFTs (non-fungible tokens), and so much more, I felt it important to address some of the legal issues and strategies that revolve around them. We do that in Chapter 6.

Chapter 7 is nobody's favorite topic but is nevertheless a crucial subject for any business owner and individual—insurance. I have many beefs with the insurance industry, but I also recognize that insurance is a critical part of everyone's asset protection strategy and is always the first line of defense.

Chapter 8 covers a topic that I'm hopeful everyone will need to reread someday as their journey of wealth accumulation reaches a point at which simple insurance and entity formation won't be enough. This chapter discusses more sophisticated and advanced asset protection strategies needed for that accumulated wealth. Even if you're not at that stage in life yet, I encourage you to read the chapter to find out what other options and strategies exist so you can put them to work for you when the time is right.

Of course, we can't have a legal strategies book without dedicating a chapter to legal strategies that should be avoided—especially given that there's so much poor advice being handed out on social media these days. Chapter 9 covers those legal strategies to avoid.

Chapter 10 wraps it all up with some little strategies that don't really warrant an entire chapter, but are important enough that everyone should be aware of them.

With that said, if you're ready to go, let's get started!

1

WE LIVE IN THE GREATEST COUNTRY IN THE WORLD, BUT...

We live in the greatest country in the world—the United States of America. Unfortunately, we also live in the most litigious country on the planet, with an alarming 40 million lawsuits filed in the United States every year.[1] That's more than 100,000 lawsuits *per day*! Yikes!

And when it comes to lawyers, it doesn't get much better. There are 1.3 million lawyers in the United States—about 1 lawyer to every 248 people in the country.[2] Compare that to 1 lawyer to 560 people in Germany, and 1 to 1,221 people in France.

These lawsuits can come from anywhere, from a simple business venture gone wrong to personal creditor claims, unexpected accidents, landlord liabilities, and even marital disputes. What's worse is that a successful lawsuit may not only cost you the assets you've accumulated over your lifetime, but they can also cost you future assets and future income if your current assets and income aren't enough to satisfy a judgment against you.

Picture this: you're late for work one morning. You hurry into your car and, stressed about time, you back out of your garage without doing your usual safety check. You fail to see a fifteen-year-old boy who is skateboarding to school and you severely injure him. Or even worse, you're driving back from work after an exhausting and extra stressful week and fail to notice that the stoplight has turned red. You accidentally run the red light, hitting a minivan driven by a mother with four children, with deadly consequences.

Maybe you own a house that you rent out. The tenant's friends come to visit and one of them slips and falls while at the house, severely injuring herself. As the property owner, you get sued. Or maybe you didn't realize that you needed to check the boiler's release valve annually and the resulting explosion severely injured your tenant and her family.

In these situations, your valuable assets—whether your home, savings, investments, W-2 income, business assets—if held in your personal name, could be directly exposed to these risks and accessible to anyone who successfully sues you and obtains a judgment against you (called a *judgment creditor*). The consequences can be financially devastating and possibly irreversible.

DEFINITION

A judgment creditor is someone who files a lawsuit against you and is successful in winning that lawsuit. When the lawsuit concludes, the judge issues a ruling that you owe the judgment creditor money. The judgment creditor then has the legal right to collect that money or enforce the terms of the judgment against you.

To make matters worse, many of these lawsuits are frivolous. They are filed by predatory attorneys who know how to game the system and who understand that most people prefer to settle to eliminate the nuisance, rather than spend years in litigation. These lawsuits will often ask for exorbitant amounts of money that greatly outweigh the damages that occurred.

Many readers will recall the lawsuit filed against McDonald's for serving extra hot coffee after a customer accidentally spilled her coffee on herself. Or maybe you've heard of the man who allegedly looked like Michael Jordan, and sued him and Nike for damages incurred due to people mistaking him for a celebrity athlete. And one of my personal favorites: the woman who sued two girls in Durango, Colorado, for medical bills relating to the stress-induced panic attack that occurred after the girls delivered cookies to her house.[3]

You might be thinking, "Yeah, but what are the odds of this really happening to me?" Well, the statistics don't lie and they aren't pretty. According to E.R. Munro and Company, you have a one in three chance of being sued at some point in your lifetime.[4] I think the number, on average, is closer to one in four or one in five, and this risk increases significantly for certain professionals. A doctor, for example, is at a much higher risk of being sued than a landlord, who's at a much higher risk of being sued than an online business. The actual statistics are very difficult to determine. However, according to the American Medical Association, one in every three physicians has been sued![5]

Even a 20 percent general risk of being sued is significant. And, when you find yourself caught up in a legal battle threatening to take away all the hard-earned assets that you've built up over the years—such as your home, rental properties, businesses, and savings —having an asset protection plan will minimize that threat and put you in the best possible position to fight and/or negotiate with the person who's trying to take it all away. Whether it's to protect yourself from lawsuits, limitations inherent in insurance policies, or just to give you peace of mind, having an asset protection plan is one of the top legal strategies that everyone can and will benefit from. This is why it's critical to understand that implementing an asset protection strategy is no longer a luxury afforded only to the rich. It's a legal strategy that everyone needs to implement.

....

Don't Have Any Assets to Protect? Think Again!

The longevity of a judgment is something many underestimate. Did you know that once a plaintiff sues you and obtains a judgment against you, in most states, the judgment is good for ten years? And did you know that when that ten years is up, the plaintiff can renew for another ten years? This means that even if you don't have many assets to protect today, if you accumulate wealth in the future, a judgment against you can hang over you for decades to come. This underscores the critical importance of robust asset protection strategies.

··

The Simple Goal of Asset Protection

Asset protection simply refers to a set of legal tools and structures used to protect your hard-earned assets (including your income) from potential creditors or legal judgments. With proper planning, these strategies can shield your wealth from various threats, thus maximizing the chances that your assets will be protected.

The conceptual goal of asset protection is fairly simple. All you're trying to do is create a separation—like constructing strong walls or safety barriers—between you and your assets. This way, we can protect *you from your assets*. And, maybe more importantly, we can also protect *your assets from you.* (Yes, you're a very dangerous person engaging in daily liability-producing activities, meaning activities that result in you getting sued, such as getting into a car accident or a business dispute.) This theme will be prevalent throughout the asset protection sections in this book.

 WARNING!

Your income is a valuable asset. A percentage of your current income—and future income—(an asset) can be taken from you by a judge in favor of a judgment creditor. Don't get caught having to work hard in the future just to pay off a judgment creditor.

Let's start with the first barrier: creating a wall to separate you from your "dangerous assets." This scenario is often referred to as an *inside attack* (see Figure 1.1).

Fig. 1.1

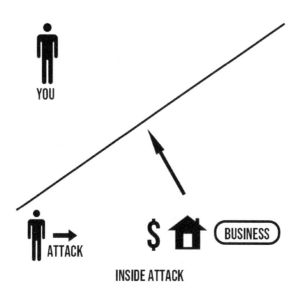

INSIDE ATTACK

An inside attack covers all the scenarios in which the assets themselves, such as your rental properties, businesses, cars, and other dangerous assets, create a liability and the injured party can make an attempt to reach you personally for those alleged liabilities. This is what most people think of when they think of asset protection. To me, this scenario is more about limiting your liability from the dangers of your assets. So, for example, if you own a piece of rental real estate, we want to make sure that if something happens to the tenant, we create barriers between your assets and you so the tenant can't sue you personally and reach your personal assets by obtaining a judgment against you.

The other side of the wall is meant to separate your assets from you. This is often referred to as an *outside attack* (see Figure 1.2).

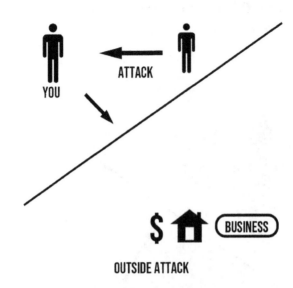

OUTSIDE ATTACK

People often forget that you're a liability-producing machine while you engage in everyday life. An outside attack refers to a situation in which something happens to you personally—unrelated to your assets—then there's a judgment against you. So if you get into a car accident or you have a dispute with someone that results in a judgment against you personally, we want to make sure that the wall prevents the judgment creditor from reaching your valuable assets on the other side of the wall.

There are several ways you can create those barriers that will make it as hard as possible for creditors who have filed lawsuits or obtained judgments against you to access your assets. A good asset protection strategy involves layering your protection. Some of you will need only one layer, while others will require many layers. Most will fall somewhere in the middle.

Why the layered approach? Because there's no single foolproof layer. Under no circumstances should you think that any one strategy will provide you with a complete defense. Each layer comes with its own set of strengths and vulnerabilities. By employing a combination of layers, you can ensure that even if one line of defense fails, others will still be in place to provide protection.

So, if you ever hear of an asset protection strategy that's "guaranteed" or "foolproof," then do yourself a favor and run as fast as you can in the opposite direction. There's no such thing as a guaranteed or foolproof strategy, and the person telling you that is simply trying to sell you something. Show me any individual layer of protection and I'll always be able to poke a hole in it. The question is, how big of a hole? Each layer adds a degree of protection, but no layer is entirely impenetrable.

 WARNING!

Never believe anyone who offers a "guaranteed" asset protection plan. Every strategy has a weakness that can be exploited. Always consult with an asset protection specialist and diversify your protection strategies.

Think of each layer of protection as a layer of clothing. If you just wear a T-shirt, this first layer may be all you need to protect you on a warm summer day, but it likely won't be enough on a cooler day, when you may also need a long-sleeved shirt. As the seasons change and it gets colder, you may need to add a sweater. Does that mean you're fully protected from the cold with those three layers? Not necessarily, because it could start to snow and you'd need to add a jacket or a heavy winter coat. That might be the best you can do, but even all those layers may not stand up to freezing, blizzard-like conditions.

Or think of medieval castle defenses. They're most effective when multiple layers of protection are in place. If a castle relied solely on its tall walls, a scaling ladder could breach them. If it depended just on its moat, a long bridge or determined swimmers could cross it. The medieval castle's strength lay in a combination of defenses: the moat to slow the advance; the walls to stop projectiles; and people, the archers, to counter those attempting to climb; and so on. Similarly, when it comes to safeguarding our most valuable assets, relying on a single strategy is a potential recipe for disaster.

Six Layers of Asset Protection

In the world of asset protection, I generally think of six layers.

LAYER 1: FREE PROTECTION

I can't think of a more basic first layer than the free variety. Certain assets are often afforded protection from creditors—either fully or up to a certain limit—depending on jurisdictional laws and regulations. It's worth noting that these protections can vary significantly by state or region. Nevertheless, you should be aware of them—especially since some may require affirmative action by you to trigger them.

Below are some assets that are commonly protected—at least in part—in many jurisdictions, particularly in the United States.

Your Home. In many states, some portion of the equity in your personal residence may be protected from creditors. This is often referred to as a homestead exemption. This protection may be automatic or you may have to make a filing with your state. Often, the protection only kicks in if you file for bankruptcy, which is rarely a desired outcome necessary to protect your home. Unfortunately, most states protect only a small amount compared to the sky-high property values these days. States such as Alabama, Illinois, and North Carolina all have protections of less than $35,000. According to the National Consumer Law Center, the primary goal of these exemptions in many states is simply "to protect consumers and their families from poverty, and to preserve their ability to be productive members of society and to recover and achieve financial rehabilitation." To be fair, some states, such as Florida, Oklahoma, and Iowa, will protect all of your home, with some exemptions.

Asset Protection Planners, which I have no affiliation with, has a great resource that lists the homestead exemption limits for all fifty states. You can check your state out at LegalStrategiesForEveryone. com/Homestead.

Retirement Funds. Federally recognized retirement accounts, such as 401(k)s and pension plans, may also be protected if they fall under the jurisdiction of a federal legislation known as the Employee Retirement Income Security Act (ERISA). Just ask O.J. Simpson—the NFL Hall of Fame football player who, according to several reports, still owes close to $100 million to the families of two people he was found liable of killing. He has been able to sidestep payments by living in Florida, where his NFL pension and the equity in his home are fully protected.

Retirement accounts that are subject to this legislation comprise 401(k)s and pension plans. However, when these funds are transferred from these plans into more prevalent Individual Retirement Accounts (IRAs) or other non-ERISA structures, the extent of their protection can vary. Your protection depends on the specific regulations of the state in which you reside.

DEFINITION

ERISA—the Employee Retirement Income Security Act. This federal law sets minimum standards for retirement and health benefit plans in private industry to provide protection for the individuals in these plans.

Wages. Although it is possible for a judgement creditor to obtain an order from the judge requiring the judgment debtor to turn over a portion of the debtor's wages to the judgment creditor, some states offer protection for a portion of the debtor's wages, ensuring that the debtor can meet basic living expenses. However, a percentage of their wages above a basic living expense is fair game. In California, for example, that's 25 percent of disposable wages.

Life Insurance. The cash value of life insurance policies may be protected from creditors in many jurisdictions. We discuss this in Chapter 7.

LAYER 2: INSURANCE

We cover the benefits of insurance in Chapter 7. Insurance is *always* the first line of defense and I highly recommend that everyone have as much insurance as they can afford. But Forbes.com highlighted the shortcomings of insurance, writing "the situations where lawsuits cause people to lose their assets typically involve a scenario where insurance coverage is insufficient and the unprotected assets owned by the defendant (i.e., you) are such that a lawyer representing the party suing you is incentivized to take a case to trial and obtain a judgment.... Unprotected assets are generally lost due to post-judgment collections."[6]

Because the benefits of insurance are often overstated, I want to spend a little time here discussing the "insufficiencies" that Forbes.com alludes to above. Again, I want to reiterate that insurance is *always* your first line of defense, and a must-have. Just don't put all your eggs in the insurance basket. Danger lies in complacently relying on insurance as the *only* layer, without considering other protective measures.

There are three main issues with insurance. The first insufficiency of insurance revolves around one of the sneakiest aspects of insurance policies—the exclusions. Exclusions in an insurance policy refer to specific conditions, situations, or circumstances under which the policy *won't* provide coverage or pay a claim. Essentially, exclusions define what *isn't* covered by the insurance policy—in other words, what's excluded from the policy. These exclusions are often subtly buried within the convoluted legalese of insurance policy documents and are the trapdoors that lead many policyholders into a false sense of security. They diligently pay their premiums every month— convinced of comprehensive coverage—only to have their claims denied when a crisis unfolds and insurance proceeds are needed.

The insurance industry, unfortunately, has gained a notorious reputation for profiting from denying claims based on these very exclusions. This forces policyholders into exhausting and time-consuming battles to get their policies to respond when they're most needed. The very structure of insurance policies makes it challenging for laymen to identify these exclusions without professional help.

As a result, I highly recommend you hire an insurance attorney to review your policy to determine what's included in and excluded from your coverage. With a clear understanding of your policy, you can make informed decisions, such as whether additional riders or addendums are necessary to bridge any potential coverage gaps. This initial investment in expert guidance could potentially save you from significant financial losses in the future.

Moving on, the second insufficiency centers on underinsurance— a common but dangerous pitfall. This isn't necessarily a failing on the part of insurance companies but rather a result of policyholders misjudging, or having a lack of foresight about the extent of coverage they might require. A coverage of $1 million or even $3 million might initially seem generous, but the sufficiency of this coverage comes into question in the face of calamitous incidents.

Consider the scenario of a serious auto accident that results in severe injuries to the passengers or even death. Your auto policy has "high" limits of $100,000 per person and $300,000 per incident. Your umbrella policy picks up the rest up to $1,000,000. But the resulting judgment due to the severity of the injuries is in the millions. In these instances, insurance coverage that seemed substantial turns out to be inadequate, leaving you exposed to potentially crippling financial liabilities.

Finally, we must address the not-so-improbable scenario of insurance companies going bankrupt. This risk is particularly prevalent with newer, internet-exclusive companies that haven't had the chance to establish a solid financial foundation. All too often, policyholders discover that their insurance company has folded just when they need to file a claim, leaving them high and dry.

Alternatively, an unexpected catastrophic event can trigger a deluge of claims, swiftly depleting an insurer's reserves. This can push them toward bankruptcy, consequently leaving policyholders without coverage. These instances underline the critical need for additional safeguards, such as entity structures or asset protection trusts (APTs), reinforcing the concept of insurance as the first—but not the only—line of defense. Entity structures and APTs are detailed in the later chapters.

In conclusion, by refraining from placing all your eggs in the insurance basket, you're not only buying yourself peace of mind, but also securing a future in which your hard-earned assets remain safeguarded from unforeseen calamities. Remember, true financial resilience doesn't lie in the illusion of comprehensive coverage, but in the reality of a well-rounded, foolproof, asset protection strategy.

LAYER 3: PRIVACY

Privacy works best when coupled with insurance. We cover privacy in Chapter 2. When privacy techniques are employed, a plaintiff's lawyer will be unable to determine whether any assets exist to go after if they're successful in obtaining a judgment. This uncertainty incentivizes them to settle claims for policy limits or for pennies on the dollar. It's simply the path of least resistance for most plaintiffs' lawyers.

LAYER 4: ENTITY STRUCTURING

"Own nothing, control everything" is the cornerstone of this fourth layer, which is also covered in Chapter 2. In the event that insurance is not sufficient because an exclusion or a claim exceeds your policy limits, entity structuring acts as a backstop to the penetrated insurance policy. It provides an additional layer of protection between the plaintiff's lawyer and your assets. However, depending on how aggressively certain state judges treat you, these entity structures have their limitations. From judges who are inclined to pierce the corporate veil to reach you personally to judges who apply the wrong state law to reach the assets held by your entities, there are many reasons why this layer is not the be-all end-all of asset protection. Having this backstop is much better than *not* having it, but there are still a lot of potential holes.

LAYER 5: APTs

Asset protection trusts are generally much stronger than simple entities, but they're expensive to set up and maintain, making them impractical for anyone other than individuals who have lots of assets to protect. Not all states recognize domestic asset protection trusts (DAPTs) and the offshore variety have a few weak spots. We cover APTs in Chapter 9.

LAYER 6: EQUITY STRIPPING

Sophisticated structures, such as equity stripping or lien/lease placements, are typically best used in conjunction with APTs or entity structuring. Together, they're like the heavy winter coat that's expensive to buy but provides you with the best possible protection. However, they're not bulletproof. We discuss equity stripping in Chapter 8.

STRATEGY

The best asset protection strategies generally involve a combination of some or all of these layers, depending on whether you're just starting out, are experienced with a lot of assets, or are a high net worth individual. This is especially true with the more advanced strategies that work best when coupled with APTs and privacy.

How and When to Implement the Six Layers of Asset Protection

Let's discuss overall timing first. How great would it be if we got into an auto accident, had a business dispute, or got sued for something, and were simply able to call around and obtain insurance to cover us for that claim? I'll tell you—it would be amazing! And we wouldn't have to bother thinking about these strategies until tragedy actually struck.

Obviously, we can't do that. And neither can we implement most of these six layers of asset protection once a claim arises, or even after you knew—or should've known—that a potential threat of a suit was out there. As John F. Kennedy so eloquently put it, "The time to repair the roof is when the sun is shining." Or, as I have heard *Rich Dad Poor Dad* author, Robert Kiyosaki say on a few occasions, "The time to put your seat belt on is before the crash."

Once the accident happens or you become aware of a potential claim, it's too late to scramble and get insurance in place or implement most of the layers described in this chapter.

Why?

Because there's a legal principle called *fraudulent conveyance* or *fraudulent transfer*. These laws prohibit you from transferring any of your assets out of your name and into one of these protective structures once you know—or should've known—about a potential claim against you. If you make transfers after the fact, fraudulent transfer laws allow judges to reverse any transfers you made or disregard entity structures. So once the harm is inflicted, it's too late.

Now let's discuss when you should generally consider each of these layers of protection.

Starting Out. If you're young or just starting out and all you have is W-2 income, then insurance is likely the only layer of protection you need. This would primarily be for protecting your future income. Remember, a judgment is valid for the next ten years and can be renewed for another ten years at that time. If you've started to accumulate some savings, own a few stocks, or maybe have purchased your first rental property, then this is the time to seriously consider adding a little entity structuring into your asset protection plan. There are pros and cons to doing this, but you should at least start thinking about adding Layers 2 and 3.

Established. Once you have significant assets to protect—such as multiple rental properties, a business that has value, or other assets—in addition to insurance, you should definitely add entity structures to separate yourself from your business and create an additional barrier between you and your assets. At this level, the discussion should center around how many entities you need rather than whether you need them at all. Chapter 10 will help you in that analysis.

High Net Worth. Once you reach a financial level at which the value of your estate is in the millions of dollars, the discussion should turn to adding APTs and more complex strategies. The more your profession exposes you to liability, the lower that financial level would be. For example, heart surgeons, lawyers, or any other profession that has a high likelihood of a lawsuit, should consider trusts much earlier in life—even if asset values are on the lower end. For example, a doctor may want to consider an APT when the value of their assets reaches $2 million, as opposed to a passive investor, who could wait until $5 million to discuss trusts.

Consequences of Not Implementing These Strategies

So what happens when you don't implement legal strategies that ultimately protect your hard-earned tangible assets or income?

Short answer: someone can take almost everything away from you!

Bank accounts, real estate, vehicles, boats, jewelry, and just about anything else of value could be seized by your creditors or an injured party if they win a lawsuit against you. If you don't have enough tangible assets to satisfy a judgment, you might be forced to turn over a portion of your wages (current and future) to that person or business until they've recouped the amount that a court has determined you owe them.

Other expected (future) assets besides wages can also be seized. These might include commissions, royalties, tax refunds, insurance payouts, stock dividends, stock options, and even certain types of trust income. Past assets that you recently transferred to someone else are vulnerable to seizure, as well.

As you work your way through this book, you'll notice that asset protection is one of its major themes. This is because I can't think of a more important legal strategy than ensuring the financial security of yourself, your family, and your legacy. I think you'll agree with me.

2

OWN NOTHING, CONTROL EVERYTHING

John D. Rockefeller, one of the richest men in history, is often credited with saying, "Own nothing, control everything." This saying may sound like a strange strategy at first, but it's actually a pretty simple concept and an easy way to increase the safety of your valuable assets, such as your savings, investments, or home.

This strategy simply involves never holding your valuable assets in your personal name. Instead, control them through separate legal entities. By doing so, you can enjoy the benefits of the asset (through control mechanisms) without the direct risk of someone taking your asset away from you in litigation or bankruptcy.

This concept has been used by the wealthy for centuries. By removing themselves from direct ownership, yet maintaining the strings of control, wealthy individuals could mitigate risks while reaping rewards. This philosophy was rooted in the desire to protect one's hard-earned assets from potential threats, such as economic downturns, predatory lawsuits, or changing political climates. In this day and age, however, everyone should use this strategy. It isn't just reserved for the wealthy anymore.

I'll go a step further and venture to say it's the most common legal strategy out there.

Why?

Because in the US legal system, liability often attaches to ownership and if you don't own something, no one can take it away from you. If you own an asset, you could be held financially responsible for claims or judgments tied to that asset. This extends across the vast spectrum of assets, from real estate and vehicles to businesses and personal property.

For example, when you go into business and provide a product or service, you'll likely bear financial responsibility for a product or service that causes harm. When you own rental real estate and someone gets injured on your property, liability attaches to the owner of the property—even if the owner wasn't directly involved—such as slip and fall due to icy sidewalks or tripping hazards. In a car accident, not only is the driver responsible for any injuries they cause, but the owner of the vehicle is also liable—especially if the owner lent the vehicle to another driver.

Some liabilities are head scratchers. For example, did you know that if you have a pool in your yard, you can be held liable if someone drowns or gets injured—even if they were trespassing and using the pool without your permission? Or if someone steals your firearm and commits a crime, you may be held liable.

All this to say that, in the United States, simple ownership of an asset creates potential liability for you that must be addressed.

One way to limit your exposure for a business, therefore, is to conduct that business through a legal entity. This way, you don't personally own the business. Your business entity does. Naturally, you remain the president or chief executive officer (CEO) of your business and you own the entity that in turn owns the actual business. But you don't own the business personally. You have incorporated your business. That way, if any dispute arises between the business and your customer, vendor, or any third party, the dispute would be with your legal entity, not with you personally.

Similarly, if you own rental property, one way to limit your exposure is to own the property in a limited liability company (LLC) since the legal owner of the property is generally liable for any claims that arise on the property. You remain in control of the LLC as the manager but, by holding the title to your rental property in an LLC, you limit your personal exposure by transferring the legal exposure to your LLC. Only assets of the LLC can be reached by the injured party.

Different Types of Entities

Before we dive into the intricacies of transferring ownership from your personal name into an entity, let's discuss what those entities are, the pros and cons of each entity, and when to use each type of entity.

Corporations. A corporation is a legal entity separate from its owners, created under the authority of a state's laws. The owners are called *shareholders* and corporations are managed and controlled through a board of directors. The board in turn elects officers such as CEOs and presidents (see Figure 2.1).

Fig. 2.1

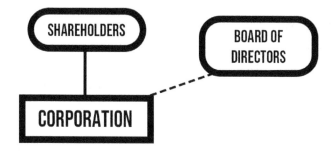

Corporations offer limited liability to its shareholders, meaning owners are typically not personally responsible for the corporation's debts and liabilities. This is why when you purchase shares such as Apple or Google in the stock market you're not personally liable for any issues that arise in one of those companies. But you don't have to be a megacorporation to enjoy this benefit. Even a small business that you incorporate with a corporation will enjoy this limitation of liability if you follow all the rules.

However, in most states, if you owe someone money and a judgment is entered against you, judges are allowed to give your judgment creditors shares in your corporation until the amount of money they're owned is satisfied. In the context of asset protection, this is one of the major drawbacks of corporations.

Corporations are also subject to specific taxation rules and often pay taxes on their profits, leading to potential double taxation when profits are distributed to shareholders as dividends. This is the primary reason we generally don't hold rental real estate in a corporation. If you were to own your real estate in a corporation, and the rental property made $100 profit for the corporation, the corporation would be taxed on that $100. Then when the corporation distributed the remaining profits to you, those profits would be taxed again on your personal tax returns.

Another reason we generally don't use corporations to own real estate is depreciation, which is one of the top benefits of owning rental real estate. With a corporation, the depreciation that the property provides would be taken at the corporation level, thereby reducing profits. However, when a dividend is paid out to the shareholders, there's no depreciation for the shareholder to claim on their personal tax returns, thus not allowing them to offset other income and reduce their personal taxes. Generally speaking, corporations are used for large businesses.

Limited Partnerships (LPs). An LP is a separate legal entity composed of at least two parties—the limited partners and the general partners. The limited partners have ownership of the entity but no control. The general partners have both the ownership of the entity *and* the control. The general partners also have unlimited liability for the debts and obligations of the entity, so it's not a desirable type of partnership to be in (see "Steer Clear of Sole Proprietorships and General Partnerships" later in this chapter). It's common to see the general partner be, in and of itself, a separate entity to add protection along with the control (see Figure 2.2).

Fig. 2.2

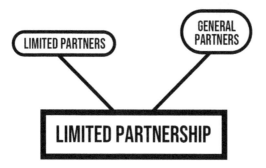

The appeal of an LP is that the limited partners have liability that's typically restricted to their investment in the LP. This means that personal assets of limited partners are shielded from the partnership's liabilities, provided they don't engage in management activities. This is why LP structures are popular with businesses that have multiple passive investors.

From a tax perspective, LPs are typically treated as pass-through entities, similar to partnerships or sole proprietorships. This means that the company's profits or losses pass through to partners' individual tax returns, avoiding the double taxation seen with some corporations. This is one of the reasons why LPs are one of the more popular entities in which to hold real estate, along with limited liability companies. They provide liability protection as well as providing for the depreciation of the real estate to pass through to the owner's personal tax return. The flexibility also makes LPs an attractive option for many entrepreneurs and business owners.

Limited Liability Company (LLC). An LLC is a popular business and asset-holding structure. The owners are called *members* and LLCs are managed and controlled by one or more managers, who can also be—and typically are—members or other entities that are owned and controlled by the members (see Figure 2.3).

Fig. 2.3

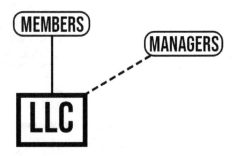

This entity is designed to provide its members with a shield against personal liability for the company's debts or legal actions. This means that members are typically not personally responsible for the company's liabilities, which protects their personal assets from potential business creditors.

From a tax perspective, LLCs have the same characteristics as LPs and are typically treated as pass-through entities.

Series LLCs. A series LLC is a unique form of LLC available only in certain parts of the United States. The standout feature of a series LLC is its ability to have separate *series* or *cells* within the over-arching LLC framework. Each series can operate almost like an independent LLC, with its own assets, operations, members, and even its own distinct business purposes (see Figure 2.4).

Fig. 2.4

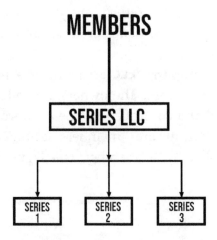

Each series, however, is not a separate legal entity and is created informally without any state filings. Similar to having multiple LLCs owned by a single parent LLC, each series potentially provides liability protection from each of the other series. The liabilities of one series are, by design, not the obligations of another series or the master LLC. This means if one series incurs a debt or faces a lawsuit, only the assets of that particular series are at risk, shielding the assets of the other series and the main LLC.

This structure can be particularly appealing to real estate investors who own multiple properties. For instance, each property could be held under a separate series, ensuring that potential liabilities associated with one property don't affect the others (see Figure 2.5).

Fig. 2.5

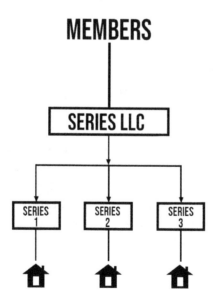

We discuss series LLCs in more detail in Chapter 9.

Trusts. When we refer to trusts in the asset protection context, we're specifically referring to APTs that are irrevocable trusts. A trust has no owners. Instead, trusts have beneficiaries who benefit from the trust, and trustees who operate and control the trust (see Figure 2.6).

Fig. 2.6

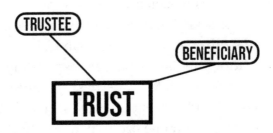

Once inside the trust, assets generally become inaccessible to future creditors, lawsuits, or judgments, provided the trust is set up and maintained correctly. We do a deep dive into APTs in Chapter 8.

PRO TIP

To maintain your limited liability status as a member of an LLC or a limited partner of an LP, you must not be involved in managing the company. If you remain as a silent partner, your liability should be limited to the amount of capital you contribute to the partnership. However, if you engage in management, you risk losing your protected status and could be treated as a general partner and, therefore, be held liable for the debts and obligations of the company.

Steer Clear of Sole Proprietorships and General Partnerships

Avoid these two types of ownership structures at all costs. They're the worst types of business structures, in terms of asset protection.

1. Sole Proprietorship. *Sole proprietors are the complete opposite of the principles of own nothing and control everything. They conduct business and own all their assets in their personal names. Some sole proprietors do business under a fictitious name to gain credibility in the marketplace and may even obtain a separate tax identification number (known as an EIN), but they have unlimited liability for acts of their business and all their assets are exposed. This is something that's often overlooked by sole proprietors who own rental property. Even if your rental property is small and has little to no equity to protect, a sole proprietor who owns the rental real estate in their personal name has unlimited exposure from the rental property.*

2. General Partnership. *Also known as a GP, this is typically worse than doing business as a sole proprietor. Why? Because not only are you personally responsible for the acts and damages of the business, you're also personally liable for the acts of your business partners. So when your partners' acts cause injury or harm, you'll be held personally responsible.*

Now that we understand all the different menu options when it comes to entity structures, we need to be aware that simply transferring the asset into one of these entities doesn't guarantee that liability stops at the entity level. We need to take additional steps to ensure that the "corporate veil" we've created isn't pierced in such a way that the entity will be disregarded and creditors can attach liability to us, personally.

Piercing the Corporate Veil

For our own nothing, control everything strategy to be success-ful, we need to do everything we can to ensure that our corporate veil remains intact. The corporate veil is the legal concept behind this strategy and separates the liabilities and obligations of an entity from its owners, shareholders, or members. This separation protects the personal assets of the owners from the debts and liabilities of the company. Essentially, the company is treated as a separate legal entity, distinct from those who own or control it (see Figure 2.7).

Fig. 2.7

But this corporate veil isn't absolute and there are ways the veil can be pierced if proper steps aren't taken to secure its integrity. Here are the five most common ways that judges pierce the corpo-rate veil of your entity and allow plaintiffs to bypass the entities to reach your personal assets.

1. Commingling Personal and Business Assets. Commingling personal and business assets is a surefire way to blur the distinction between your personal finances and the finances of your business, and quickly leads to the corporate veil being ignored. This can be as simple as using a business bank account for personal expenses or vice versa, or using a business asset for personal use. Proper separation of assets is fundamental in maintaining the protective shield offered by the corporate veil. When these boundaries are breached, it may provide grounds for courts to pierce the corporate veil and hold owners personally liable for business debts. So always maintain separate accounts and meticulously document each transaction.

2. Failure to Observe Corporate Formalities. Corporate formalities include holding regular meetings, keeping accurate minutes, and making clear resolutions. Following these formalities helps validate the separation between you and your entity. Skipping these steps can give the impression that the business isn't as genuine, and you're not treating the entity as independent, but rather as an extension of your personal affairs. This is another surefire way for your corporate veil to be invalidated by a judge.

3. Undercapitalization. Not providing enough capital for the business to meet its foreseeable obligations can invalidate the corporate veil. If a company is deliberately underfunded, and that leads to insolvency or the inability to cover liabilities, courts might view this as an abuse of the corporate structure. This is one of the reasons why having a sufficient insurance policy for the entity is so important—because it counters the argument that there was insufficient capital for the entity.

4. Fraud. Using the entity to commit fraud and other wrongful acts.

5. Alter Ego. Similar to commingling funds, operating a company as an "alter ego" means treating it as an extension of your personal affairs rather than as a separate legal entity. When this occurs, the lines between personal and business actions and finances blur. If you don't respect the distinct boundaries, you risk the dissolution of the corporate veil. Courts, in such cases, may determine that the business doesn't function as a genuine entity. If so, the protective barrier against personal liability dissolves, making you personally liable for company debts.

Outside Attacks

Up until now, we've focused on only half of the strategy. That is, to protect ourselves from our assets, we must remove ownership and hold the asset in a favorable entity, maintaining the corporate formalities to minimize the changes that can occur when the corporate veil is pierced. But recall in Chapter 1 that we talked about how there's another angle to this problem. Not only must we protect ourselves from our dangerous assets (which we call an *inside attack* and has been the subject of this chapter, so far) but we also must protect our assets from ourselves. In the section in Chapter 1 called "The Simple Goal of Asset Protection," we referred to this as *outside attacks*.

Let's go back to the scenario mentioned in Chapter 1. You're late for work one morning. You hurry into your car and, stressed about time, you back out of your garage without doing your usual safety check. You fail to realize that a fifteen-year old boy is skateboarding to school and you severely injure him. Let's call him Skateboarder Sam, as we'll be referring to him often in this book. Skateboarder Sam's parents file a lawsuit against you and receive a judgment in court for a significant amount that far exceeds the actual damages that you believe were reasonable. Your insurance policy only covers a portion of the damages, so Skateboarder Sam's attorney now brings you into a judgment debtor examination, where he's allowed to ask you all kinds of questions about which assets you own, including LLCs, corporations, rental real estate, and where they're located. Because you're under oath, you must disclose all of this information.

The attorney discovers that you own two rental properties that have sufficient equity in them to cover the remainder of the judgment. The problem for the attorney, however, is that you've legally created an LLC and the properties aren't owned in your personal name, but instead are owned by the LLC. So the attorney goes to the judge and requests that you turn over the ownership of the LLCs to her client.

This is what we consider an outside attack—an attack on your real estate assets that has nothing to do with the underlying claim, which was you injuring Skateboarder Sam. A similar situation would arise if you had a business dispute that resulted in a judgment against you personally and the attorney wanted to go after the assets in your LLC.

Charging Order Protection

There are several legal options that a judge could have. The worst case scenario would be that the judge orders you to turn your ownership in the LLC over to the judgment creditor. If that happened, you'd lose control and ownership of the LLC and the judgment creditor would likely liquidate the real estate to satisfy the judgment. Another option would be for the judge to put a lien on your rental property so that you couldn't sell or refinance the property without first satisfying the judgment lien.

But in a perfect world, the judge will limit Skateboarder Sam to what's called a *charging order*. When a judge issues a charging order instead of a turnover order or a lien, you don't have to turn over the ownership of the LLC or the management of the LLC. All you have to do is hand any distributions you would've received from your LLC over to the judgment creditor until the creditor's judgment is satisfied. In other words, the charging order limits the creditor to intercepting distributions that might otherwise have been made to you.

This arrangement has two benefits for you—the LLC owner. First, you don't have to give ownership or control over to the judgment creditor. So you're free to continue operating your business or rental real estate as usual, without fear of interference from the judgment creditor, who doesn't care about your business and just wants to liquidate everything to get paid. Second—and more importantly—because you retain management and control over your LLC, you're able to stop making distributions to yourself. After all, why would you make distributions to yourself if all that money is simply going to go to your judgment creditor?

This frustrates the judgment creditor (and their attorney even more, since they can't get paid) and puts you in a much stronger position to negotiate a settlement and discount the judgment—or at the very least, enter into a reasonable payment plan. It also generally encourages plaintiffs" lawyers to settle claims before a judgment is even obtained, due to the perceived difficulties with collection when they eventually get a judgment. There are alternative ways that you may be able to get money out of your LLC that don't involve a distribution, which is the actual target of the lien.

Now to be clear, not all states provide charging order protection as the exclusive remedy, so it's important to know how your particular state addresses this issue and to have a good asset protection attorney to structure it properly. California and Georgia, for example, are probably two of the worst asset protection states out there. So if a California judge has jurisdiction over your case, then the judge can award any of the three options. Conversely, about half of the states insist that charging order protection is the sole remedy available to the judgment debtor.

PRO TIP

Single-member LLCs (those that only have one owner) present their own challenges because charging order protection was really designed to protect business partners, which are nonexistent with a single-member LLC. As of the writing of this book, only five states officially provided charging order protection to single-member LLCs: Alaska, Delaware, Nevada, Texas, and Wyoming. If you reside in any of those states, then register your LLC in your state. More on this is discussed in Chapter 9.

Putting It All Together

Let's put what we've learned into some specific examples to wrap this up and put it into practical application.

Let's assume Bob is in his mid-forties and has accumulated a little bit of wealth from a small business he has built over the past fifteen years. He has some savings in a bank, a personal residence, a brokerage account, and some rental properties (see Figure 2.8).

Fig. 2.8

BOB

Based on our analysis above, there are two scenarios (or attacks) that we're generally concerned with: the inside attack and the outside attack.

Inside Attacks: The first concern is that something happens that directly relates to one of the assets or businesses that Bob owns. Let's say a tenant slips and falls at one of his rental properties. As the owner of that rental property, he'd be legally liable for any injuries sustained by that tenant on his property. Or perhaps he and one of his customers has a dispute that results in substantial economic or physical harm. Then, as the business owner, he'd be personally liable for those losses.

These inside attacks are represented in Figure 2.9.

Fig. 2.9

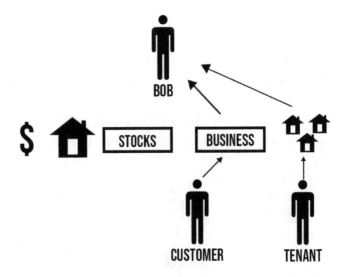

Outside Attacks: The second concern is that something happens to Bob that has nothing to do with any of the assets he owns. I didn't tell you earlier, but it was actually Bob who injured Skateboarder Sam and a judgment was entered against him for an amount higher than his insurance would cover.

This outside attack is represented in Figure 2.10.

Fig. 2.10

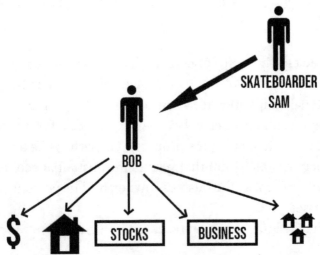

RENTAL PROPERTIES

By implementing the own nothing, control everything strategy, Bob would've been wise to create a separate LLC for each property. By transferring the ownership in his properties into the LLCs that he owns, and respecting the corporate formalities of the LLC, Bob's liability should be limited if anything were to happen to one of those properties. The corporate veil would prevent an injured tenant, for example, from pursuing damages against anyone other than the owner, which is the LLC (see Figure 2.11).

Fig. 2.11

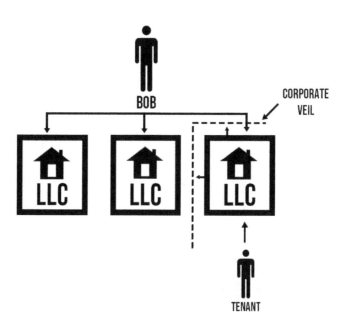

But remember, this is only half the equation. Although the LLCs should provide limited liability to Bob, we still need to be concerned about the liability that arises when Bob injures Skateboarder Sam and the court awards a judgment. That incident has nothing to do with these two rental properties. If either of these properties are located in states that don't have charging order protection as the exclusive remedy (as discussed above), those LLCs (and the properties they own) can be taken away from Bob.

Bob would be wise to set up an LLC in a state, such as Wyoming, where charging order protection is the exclusive remedy available to Skateboarder Sam. Bob doesn't have to live in the state where he creates his LLCs, and neither do you. By setting up an LLC in Wyoming, Bob would no longer own the properties and would no longer own LLCs in states that don't protect him. So Bob would be wise to own a Wyoming LLC that, in turn, owned the two property LLCs, availing himself of both the corporate veil and the charging order protection (see Figure 2.12).

Fig. 2.12

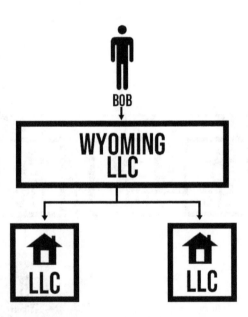

A final word. There's still a risk that a court could decide to apply the laws of a state that aren't favorable to us, which is a big reason why we use layers. The next layer (the heavy winter coat) is discussed in Chapter 8.

INVESTMENTS

Remember, anything that Bob owns in his personal name is available to satisfy the judgment that Skateboarder Sam's attorney obtained against him. The easiest assets to find and attach are cash and brokerage accounts. In fact, this is basically publicly available information since the attorney can hire bank and brokerage search services to find out how much cash Bob has. The attorney likely found this information even before he filed the lawsuit.

It would be wise for Bob to create an LLC and open a bank account and brokerage account in the name of that LLC. That way, not only will a bank search not turn it up, but he would no longer personally own the cash—it would instead be owned by the LLC. Where should Bob set up that LLC? You guessed it—in Wyoming or any of the other favorable states.

BUSINESS

Bob would be wise to follow similar principles for his business as he did for his rental properties, which, after all, are a form of business. Although businesses are often structured as corporations, I personally recommend that Bob set up his business as an LLC, then have it taxed as a corporation (or S corp). That's the beauty of LLCs—they have major tax flexibility and can be taxed however you want. The added benefit is charging order protection, as this essential asset protection law isn't available to corporations. Finally, Bob could consider stripping away the valuable assets of the business with a lien or a lease. Both strategies are discussed in in Chapter 8. The main reason for considering the next layer is that the business is really stuck with the laws of the state that it's doing business with. So if Bob lived in California, owned a business (or asset) in California, and the injury or harm occurred in California, Bob would have an uphill battle to have any other state's law apply to his situation. So if the charging order protection isn't available, it's best that the business not own any valuable assets but instead lease them from another of Bob's LLCs, as discussed in Chapter 8.

It's As Easy as Step-by-Step

Looking for a step-by-step process for accomplishing the own nothing, control everything strategy? Read on.

Step 1: Create an Entity. *The most common entity used today is an LLC. File the articles of organization with your state's secretary of state. use an attorney or a company to file this for you so your name, as the organizer, doesn't appear in the public records. Use a professional registered agent so that your personal information isn't used. The attorney or company should draft the operating agreement so that it contains the appropriate legal safeguards. For a list of questions you should ask yourself before you set up your entity, you can watch "8 Questions to Ask BEFORE You Set Up Your LLC" at LegalStrategiesForEveryone.com/8Questions.*

Step 2: Obtain an EIN. *Every LLC should obtain an EIN in order to open a separate bank account in the name of the LLC. All income and expenses of the new LLC should be run through that separate bank account. Even if you're simply holding an asset and conducting no business (such as owning an LLC, cash, or precious metals), get a bank account anyway. It's the easiest way to show the world that you're separate from your LLC.*

Step 3: Transfer the Asset into the LLC. *If you own rental property, you'll need to file a deed with the county recorder's office in the county where the property is located. Make sure that the ownership of the LLC matches the ownership of the property before the transfer. That way, according to the guidance issued by both Fannie Mae and Freddie Mac, lenders should not enforce their due-on-sale clause. For a copy of these guidelines, visit LegalStrategiesForEveryone.com/Due OnSale. If you plan to hold other LLCs inside the new LLC, prepare a document transferring the underlying LLC ownership from your personal name to the new LLC name.*

Step 4: Corporate Formalities. *Make sure that you're conforming with the corporate formalities as described in the section "Piercing the Corporate Veil" in this chapter.*

Added Benefit of This Strategy: Privacy

One of the by-products of the own nothing, control everything strategy is privacy—one of the more overlooked legal strategies when it comes to asset protection. By transferring assets into separate legal entities, it's also possible to hide from public view the amount of the assets you truly possess.

To be clear, privacy in and of itself doesn't have asset protection magical powers. You should be able to show your entire asset protection structure to a judge and feel comfortable that you've legally maximized your protection. But if your assets can't be found, it discourages lawyers from even suing you in the first place. Even if they do sue you, it encourages attorneys to settle for insurance limits.

Here is why.

Personal injury lawyers work on a contingency fee basis, meaning they only get paid if they recover money for their clients. So the first thing a plaintiff's lawyer is going to do is an asset search on you before they ever consider taking on a plaintiff's case. They'll do a bank search, a brokerage account search, and a property search on you—any public search that can yield information about which assets you possess. If the attorney can't determine which you own, or where and how you own it, they have less of an incentive to take on the case against you.

Litigation is expensive and time consuming, and if the attorney believes that they'll have difficulty identifying and accessing your assets, they might reconsider the practicality of legal action. The last thing an attorney wants to do is spend the next three years of their life working on winning a case against you, only to find out there's no money at the end of the road.

You see, most people don't realize that our civil justice system actually consists of two phases. First is the work you put in to obtain a judgment against the other side. But the second—and more important phase—is actually collecting on that judgment. Two completely different procedures. And here's the kicker: your ability to pay a judgment is completely irrelevant while in the first phase of the process, meaning a plaintiff can't force you to reveal what assets you have.

As a result, attorneys must wait until after a judgment is obtained to ask you questions (under oath) about what assets you own and what entities are yours. This is done during a judgment debtor examination.

So put yourself in the shoes of a plaintiffs" attorney. Would you spend your own money, resources, and time working for free for several years to obtain a judgment only to find out there's nothing to collect at the end of the journey? This is why attorneys typically recommend settling for policy limits or don't even take the case if they're told no insurance is available.

I have firsthand experience with this strategy. Between college and law school, I briefly worked for a very well-known plaintiff attorney in the San Francisco Bay Area. And when I say "well-known," I'm saying he advertised through late-night TV commercials. I was responsible for fielding our incoming calls from people who wanted us to take on their injury claims. One of the things I learned while working at the law office was that the first thing we did before taking on a case was to find out whether the potential defendant had insurance and, more specifically, what type of insurance they had. Some insurance companies are notorious for being difficult to deal with from a claimant's perspective (great for you as the insured). After figuring out the insurance situation, we'd move on to an asset search. We wanted to make sure that their assets or insurance were sufficient to pay whatever judgment we could get against the potential defendant. If we couldn't find anything, we'd pass on the case, no matter how rock solid it was. If we weren't assured of collection at the end of the process, we wouldn't bother.

To sum this up, prior to litigation, privacy can sometimes prevent lawsuits from even happening since litigants don't want to spend time and money going after someone who doesn't appear to own much. More importantly, once litigation starts, litigants are more likely to settle for policy limits if there are no apparent assets available for collection above and beyond the insurance policy.

Here are some mini strategies you can use to implement privacy in your asset protection plan.

Cash. Instead of holding your excess cash in your personal bank account, create an LLC in a state such as Wyoming where it's next to impossible to trace the LLC back to you. Then open a business bank account and hold your excess cash in that LLC. That way, when someone does a bank search under your name, they won't find your excess cash.

PRO TIP

While most of your cash should be kept in an LLC, keep a small balance in your personal name so that when the attorney does an asset search, they find your personal bank account with a small amount of money in it. If the search finds no bank accounts, that's very unusual and may raise suspicions since everyone has a bank account these days.

Brokerage Accounts. This is a similar strategy. Open a business brokerage account in the name of a private LLC. Anyone searching for brokerage accounts in your name won't find your business account. If you already have a personal account, some brokerage firms will allow you to transfer the business brokerage account into your personal account. If they don't, you'll need to wait until you sell your stocks in your personal account before buying new stocks in the business account in order to avoid any adverse tax consequences.

Rental Property. This one is a little trickier. If you're buying property with a commercial loan, the bank will allow you to close directly in the name of the LLC, thus creating privacy. Also, residential properties that are purchased with cash, a loan from a hard money lender, or through smaller regional banks may also be purchased directly inside an LLC. The challenge with smaller rental properties (one to five units) is that most lenders won't allow you to close in the name of your LLC, so you'll have to transfer the property into the LLC later. This, unfortunately, not only creates a paper trail (in the county recorder's office), but the loan in your personal name also remains on the books.

PRO TIP

Even if you lose privacy this doesn't mean you shouldn't transfer the property into your LLC. You'll still benefit from the asset protection, even if you don't have the privacy.

DEFINITION

A hard money lender makes loans secured by real estate as collateral and doesn't require the borrower to have creditworthiness. The lender strictly relies on the income of and equity in the property itself. These loans typically have a higher interest rate than a more traditional loan from a bank.

Management Company. Set up a management company in a private state, such as Wyoming. It's virtually impossible to trace ownership or management in Wyoming. List the management company as the manager of your LLC in whichever state you create your LLC. Most states require only the manager information and the registered agent information be listed in the public records. By using a professional third-party registered agent and a private management company, you avoid listing your personal information in the public records.

Nominee Services. When setting up entities, to avoid having to put your personal information in the public records, you can hire a nominee. The nominee is listed as the manager or officer in the public records, then resigns after the filing, thereby reinstating you as the manager or officer. It's also a good idea to use a professional registered agent service to be named as the registered agent of your entity, as opposed to having your own name on it.

Use Professional Registered Agents. All entities must provide to the public records the name and address of an individual or company that's legally authorized to receive legal papers on behalf of the company. This registered agent must be physically located in the state where the company is created. By using a professional registered agent, your personal name remains off the public records.

Don't Organize the Entity Yourself. The organizer is the person who actually files the paperwork with the secretary of state. if you do this yourself, your name will appear on the public records as the organizer. To avoid this, use an attorney or an incorporating service to file your paperwork with the state.

Naming Entities. Don't name entities with your name, the name of your children, or your favorite sports team, if you'd prefer the entities to remain private. Name your entities in such a way that they have no connection to you—*if* you want privacy, that is.

A word of caution when it comes to privacy. While privacy is a powerful tool, it's essential to approach it ethically. It shouldn't be used to deceive, evade taxes, or engage in illegal activities. Transparency with tax authorities is critical. The goal of privacy in asset protection isn't about hiding from legitimate debts or responsibilities, but rather about creating a barrier against unwarranted claims and predatory actions.

3

DON'T LEAVE YOUR CHILDREN HANGING BY LETTING THE GOVERNMENT TELL YOU WHAT TO DO

I get it. Nobody wants to think about the day they die, especially early on in their life. This is probably why a 2021 Gallup poll found that at least 54 percent of American adults have no will.[7] Here's the problem: *everyone* has a will, whether they want one, need one, or are even aware of it.

The problem is if you don't create a will yourself, the government will decide where your assets will be distributed and who'll take care of your children, pets, and treasured family photos and possessions. This generic will that the government uses is located in your state's "trust and will" statute. So if you haven't yet created a will, you can check out what your will actually says—right now.

The will drafted for you by the government is not only one that you didn't draft yourself, but it also comes at a cost to implement and an order of distribution that you may not agree with or like. Even if the distribution goes to the people you want (i.e., your parents), the legal process of how those distributions get made (known as the *probate process*) is costly and may eat up most—if not all—of your assets and/or belongings, especially if you don't have many.

But here is the worst thing you can do: have no will when you have children or other dependents. If both you and your spouse meet an untimely death, and you have no will, then the government will decide what's "in the best interest" of your children and decide who should take care of them. I don't know of any parent who consciously wants a judge or a government bureaucrat determining who their children get to go stay with after the already traumatic experience of losing their parents.

In some cases, if family members aren't available or are deemed unfit, the government can appoint a nonrelative to take care of your children. If no one suitable is found, the government may make your children wards of the state, and child protective services or a similar government agency might step in.

Even when family members are available, maybe you want your children to go live with your parents. But what about your spouse's parents? What if your parents are divorced? What about your sister, their aunt? It gets complicated and everyone's situation is unique. But taking the time to document your wishes in a will helps make your children's transition easier.

Assuming you have children and took out a life insurance policy, as will be discussed in Chapter 7, how do you want that money to be allocated to your children? All at once? Over time? With some conditions? How much of that money should go to the new legal guardian to assist with their care? Should you invest the money and have your children live off the interest? When my wife and I became parents, we painstakingly and openly talked about all these issues and how we wanted our children to live and be financially supported in the case of our death.

One of the hardest things, I've found, is not wanting your children to come into a large sum of money (via a life insurance policy, for example) that will take away their incentive to go create their own path in life and wealth. On the other hand, they're your children and the desire to have money make up for your absence is huge. I don't think there's a right answer, but I believe every parent should think this through.

But a will is just the beginning. A proper estate plan isn't just about distributing assets. It's about ensuring your voice, values, and wishes are heard and honored, even when you're no longer around. A good estate plan also should mitigate and save on estate taxes. Don't leave these vital decisions to the government.

WARNING

Without a personally crafted will, you leave the distribution of your assets—and, more importantly, the decision about who cares for your children—up to the government's generic plan. This might not reflect your true wishes or benefit your loved ones in the way you intend. Secure your legacy by drafting your own will.

Probate Court

Whether you have a will or not, probate is the legal process your heirs must go through when you don't have a living trust. The court system must verify and oversee the execution of the will. In other words, the loved ones who you referenced in your will to get the assets and belongings you left behind don't get those assets automatically. Your wishes must be administered and approved by the court.

There are generally three downsides to going through the probate process.

First, because the will needs to go through a judge, probate is a drawn-out process involving governmental oversight. Generally, for a straightforward estate, probate can stretch for twelve to eighteen months, delaying your loved ones from accessing their inheritance. And if you're a real estate investor who owns properties in several states, separate probates may become necessary for each state, further complicating matters. So your heirs have to wait a significant length of time to get access to what they inherited from you.

Second, probate is costly. Your assets and possessions can get substantially drained by court-appointed attorney fees and court costs. I'm going to give you an example for probate here in California, where I live. I understand that this may be on the higher side and your state may not be as costly, but it gives you a sense of what expenses are out there.

California is one of the states in which statutory fees for attorneys and executors are calculated as a percentage of the gross (not net) value of the probate estate. (Remember, your estate is basically all your assets and liabilities that you had at the time of death). This means even if you owe money on a piece of real estate, the entire appraised value is used to calculate the fee, not the equity value.

Here's a general breakdown of how statutory attorney's fees are calculated in California for regular probate proceedings:

- **4 percent of the first $100,000 of the gross value of the probate estate**
- **3 percent of the next $100,000**
- **2 percent of the next $800,000**
- **1 percent of the next $9 million**
- **0.5 percent of the next $15 million**
- **For estates larger than $25 million, a reasonable amount is determined by the court.**

So, for example, if the estate's gross value is $1 million, the fee would be calculated as

- **$4,000 (4 percent of the first $100,000)**
- **$3,000 (3 percent of the next $100,000)**
- **$16,000 (2 percent of the next $800,000)**

This totals $23,000 for attorney's fees alone. Executors can receive the same amount, meaning the estate could potentially pay $46,000 for a $1 million gross estate.

In addition to these fees, there are other costs associated with probate, including but not limited to, court filing fees, appraisal fees, publication fees, bonds (if not waived in the will) and miscellaneous fees (copies, postage, etc.).

This all assumes that no one challenges the will because, if they do, the challenge complicates things and adds more legal fees. States other than California are likely less expensive, but there's an appreciable cost associated with the probate process that's better avoided.

Finally, probate lacks privacy, turning personal financial details into public records, as evidenced by celebrities such as Robin Williams, Prince, and Aretha Franklin, whose financial details posthumously became public knowledge since they all ended up going through the probate process.

The solution to avoiding probate is to create a well drafted, professional, revocable living trust, which is discussed in more detail below.

I must admit, when I hired my estate planning attorney to put my estate plan together, I was thinking that the estate plan would include a will and a living trust. To my amazement, the binder that was prepared for me contained ten documents!

This was eye-opening, so I decided to get educated on why I needed all those documents. What I quickly realized was that if these documents weren't in place, the state government would decide how my assets got distributed and who would take care of my children.

What follows is a list and description of the documents my estate planning attorney prepared for me.

Last Will and Testament

This is a legal document that dictates how your individual assets will be distributed upon your death, and your wishes for your possessions and dependents. During the will planning process, you can name your beneficiaries, designate guardians for minor children and pets, and identify the executor of your estate. An executor is the person who'll be responsible for carrying out your wishes, as outlined in your will.

After you've decided who gets your possessions, next to consider is who you'd like to care for any dependents at the time of your death. These dependents may include minor children, a loved one with special needs, aging parents under your care, or even your beloved family pets. It's essential to name a guardian in your estate plan to look after your dependents. Otherwise, as mentioned earlier, the government will appoint guardians for your dependents, whether you think they're in the best interests of your children or not.

But before you name a guardian, make sure you talk to the person ahead of time to get their consent. Remember, it doesn't have to be the same person who's going to manage your child's inheritance. You can name a third party, such as a trustee, to oversee money or assets until your child is old enough to manage their inheritance themselves or they reach a stage in their life that you've designated.

For example, many parents opt to give their children a portion of their inheritance when they turn eighteen, another portion when they turn thirty-five, and another portion at forty-five. This protects your children from squandering all their inheritance at a young age. Other parents put conditions on the inheritance. For example, a portion of the inheritance is released if the child attends college, graduates college, gets married, etc. The point isn't to discuss the specifics here, but rather to emphasize the importance of going through this exercise ahead of time.

One thing to always consider when naming a couple as co-guardians is that it could get tricky if the couple divorces. Talk to your estate planning attorney about how to prepare for this possibility. Finally, consider naming a backup guardian for your dependents, just in case your first choice isn't able to physically care for them or dies before you do, which is sometimes an issue when older parents are named and the trust isn't periodically reviewed and updated.

STRATEGY

*Regularly update your will and living trust, especially
after major life events (marriage, children, buying
property) to reflect your current wishes. This will also
considerably reduce the chances of challenges to the will
by your beneficiaries and/or heirs.*

Revocable Living Trust

A revocable living trust is a separate legal entity that holds your
assets and can help you avoid probate. As discussed earlier in this
chapter, probate is a long, drawn-out, and costly process that's
very important to avoid. In my opinion, having just a will is a great
first step, but I believe that everyone should also have a revocable
living trust.

Why?

Because a living trust is a legal tool that allows you to place
assets, such as your money, property, business, or investments,
into a separate entity. While you're alive, you maintain control (as
the trustee of the living trust) over everything in the trust, making decisions about those assets as you see fit. In the event of your
passing, the living trust sidesteps the probate process, ensuring
that your chosen successor trustee can distribute the assets to your
beneficiaries as you directed. Essentially, it offers a streamlined
way to ensure that your possessions are managed and passed on
according to your wishes.

Parties to a Trust

Settlor/Grantor: *This is you—the person who creates the trust and designates all the parties and how your estate should be administered. You decide which assets should go into the trust, how the trust should operate, and for whose benefit it should be managed. The settlor establishes the trust for the purpose of managing their assets while they're alive, and how assets will be distributed and guardians appointed upon their death.*

Trustee(s): *This is also generally you and, if you're married, your spouse—although it's possible for just one of you to be the trustee. The trustee manages and administers the trust while you're alive. You also designate your successor trustee, who takes over the role of trustee once you and your spouse are deceased. The successor trustee carries out the trust's terms, distributing assets to beneficiaries, and wrapping up the trust's affairs.*

Beneficiaries: *These are the individuals or institutions that you designate as the ones who'll receive your assets. While you're alive, you can be the primary beneficiary of the trust. After you die, the assets or income from the trust will be distributed to the designated beneficiaries, which can include family, friends, charities, or other entities.*

The sole purpose of your revocable living trust is to avoid probate. Many investors and businesspeople believe that a living trust has some asset protection value but, as we discussed briefly in the last chapter, that's a big misconception.

The trust is revocable because the grantor (you) can make changes or dissolve the trust at any time. But unlike probate, assets within the trust pass directly to beneficiaries upon the grantor's death with minimal delays and substantially less cost. Granted you have to pay a little more for a trust on the front end, but that cost is just a fraction of what it costs to die without one.

Durable Power of Attorney (DPOA)

In the event of death, your financial obligations continue. Your mortgage still needs to be paid, your credit card bills, utilities, and your bank accounts still need to be managed, and all other financial obligations continue. In addition, personal decisions also need to be made. There's no pause or forgiveness due to a tragic and untimely death. Enter the DPOA.

A DPOA is a vital legal document that allows you to select someone, often termed an *agent* or *attorney-in-fact*, to handle your financial and personal matters. This authority comes into play if, for some reason, you're unable to manage these affairs yourself. The term *durable* is especially important: it indicates that this power remains active, even if you become mentally incapacitated. By having a DPOA, you ensure that financial and personal decisions are made by someone you trust. This document offers peace of mind in knowing that, should unforeseen circumstances arise, your chosen individual will be there to act in your best interests.

Healthcare Power of Attorney (HPOA)

Similar to the DPOA, an HPOA designates someone you trust to make healthcare decisions on your behalf if you become incapacitated. Imagine you're in a situation, maybe from an accident or illness, where you're unable to tell doctors what you want. The person you've chosen in your HPOA, often called your *agent* or *proxy*, steps in to speak for you. They'll follow any guidelines or wishes you've shared with them. So, it's crucial to choose someone who knows you well and who understands your values. It's also important to have conversations with them about what you'd want in various situations. The HPOA ensures that even if you can't voice your medical preferences, you still have a say in your treatment through someone you trust.

Advanced Health Care Directive

This document outlines your wishes regarding end-of-life medical care. It can specify treatments you want or don't want to receive in certain situations. It's akin to a road map for doctors. If you ever end up in a situation in which you can't speak or let others know what you want regarding medical care, this document spells it out for them. Think of it as writing down the rules for a game, but the game is how you're treated when you're seriously ill. You can be specific, saying things such as, "If my heart stops, I don't want machines to keep it beating," or more general, such as, "I want to be as pain-free as possible." It's all about making sure you get the medical care you desire, even if you can't verbally communicate it. By setting up an Advanced Health Care Directive, you give your loved ones and medical team clarity and guidance on how to respect your wishes when it truly matters.

Health Insurance Portability and Accountability Act (HIPAA) Authorization

The HIPAA is a set of rules that protects your medical information, making sure it stays private. However, there might be times when you want certain people, such as your spouse, family, or a close friend, to access that information. The HIPAA Authorization is like giving them a temporary key to your information. It allows the people you trust to see your health records and make informed decisions for you, if needed. By filling out this form, you're making sure that the right people have the right information at the right time, especially when you can't speak for yourself.

DEFINITION

*Although most people think of an estate plan as just
a will or a living trust, it's much more than that, often
including about a dozen documents that ensure
your loved ones are fully taken care of and the odds
of disputes among your potential heirs is kept to a
minimum.*

Letter of Intent

This is a more personal document that may not be legally binding.
While it may not have the strong force of law behind it like some
official documents, it's your chance to convey specific instructions,
wishes, or important information for loved ones. For example, you
might use this letter to describe the kind of funeral or memorial
service you'd prefer. It's a way to communicate things that might
not fit into the more formal legal documents but are still crucial for
your loved ones to know.

Beneficiary Designations

Certain assets, such as life insurance or retirement accounts, are
passed to beneficiaries outside of a will or trust. It's crucial to
ensure these designations are updated and align with one's overall
estate plan.

Guardianship Designations

This is a simple yet critical document if you have minor children or dependents. This document lets you choose who'll care for your children if you're not able to. It's super important because, without this document, the decision could be left up to courts and they might pick someone you wouldn't have. But before you name a guardian, make sure you talk to the person ahead of time to get their consent, as we discussed in the "Last Will and Testament" section, above.

Digital Asset Trust or Will

With the increasing importance of online presence, some people also include provisions related to digital assets, such as e-mail accounts, social media, and digital currencies. We discuss this in more detail in Chapter 6.

Special Needs Trust

For families with a disabled loved one, this trust ensures the individual continues to receive care without jeopardizing their government benefits.

....

Drafting a Will Checklist

Here are a few steps to consider when drafting a will:

- ✓ **Determine your assets:** *Make a list of your assets, including any property, financial accounts, personal possessions, and insurance policies.*

- ✓ **Choose an executor:** *Select someone you trust to serve as the executor of your will. The executor will be responsible for* *carrying out the provisions of your will and ensuring that your assets are distributed according to your wishes.*

✓ **Identify your beneficiaries:** *Decide who you want to inherit your assets and specify their names and relationships in your will.*

✓ **Appoint a guardian:** *If you have minor children, appoint a guardian to care for them in the event of your death. Don't leave your children's fate to the government.*

✓ **Sign and witness your will:** *Make sure your will is properly signed and witnessed in accordance with your state's laws.*

It's always a good idea to consult with a lawyer or other legal professional to help you draft a will and ensure that it's legally valid and accurately reflects your wishes.

....

It may seem like a daunting task, especially since most of us don't like to think about our premature demise. But think about your children. It's worth the time and expense to get this handled today. It's also important to remember that these documents and your estate plan are fluid documents. As life evolves, so should your estate plans. Regularly revisiting and updating these documents ensures that they remain reflective of your current situations and desires. A review of your estate plan is generally recommended after a major life event such as the birth of a child or the death or marriage of a contemplated beneficiary.

Estate planning is not merely an exercise for the wealthy. It's an essential step for everyone, especially if they have children or dependents. Take control over these decisions and don't let the government tell you who gets your hard-earned wealth and, more importantly, who gets to take care of your minor children.

4

DON'T GIVE YOUR MONEY
TO LAWYERS!

We all waste money on dumb things. Unused gym memberships or subscription services come to mind. Paying late fees because you're disorganized, or buying more groceries than needed and allowing them to expire or spoil are also complete wastes of money. (I'm talking about myself, of course.)

And when it comes to legal fees, my experience is that most people waste money when deciding to use (or not use) an attorney. Now to be clear, I'm not saying you shouldn't pay or use lawyers. I'm emphasizing not wasting or spending more money than you absolutely have to.

There are three main ways you can waste money with lawyers. First, spending money on lawyers when you don't have to because there are free or cheap alternatives. Second, spending more money than you have to, meaning instead of paying $500, you pay $1,000. And third, when you don't implement a legal strategy, such as asset protection, an alternative dispute route, or some other strategy that avoids future legal fees altogether.

Let me explain a common way people throw money away with lawyers: not being prepared. Most attorneys charge for their time by the hour. According to USLegal.com and other related websites, most lawyers charge between $100 and $300 an hour. To be more specific, attorneys charge in six- or fifteen-minute blocks of time.

So, if a lawyer charges $250 an hour, that one e-mail you sent that your attorney responded to will cost you a minimum of $25 or possibly $62.50, depending on if they charged you for six or fifteen minutes. What I see all too often is people using lawyers to educate them on basic legal principles that they've never heard of before, when that information is readily available and easily found online.

If you're speaking with an asset protection attorney, for example, you shouldn't be asking the attorney what a charging order is. Plenty of resources exist online that you can use to learn and understand this concept yourself. Google "charging order protection" and hundreds of reputable law firms' websites will pop up with the answer. For free! Your job is to get your mind around these concepts so that when you have a call with your attorney you don't waste precious time paying a high hourly wage for someone to teach you legal concepts. That's just an expensive teacher. You want to save your time to ask about strategies and how to implement these principles or, at the very least, confirm that your understanding is correct as opposed to having the attorney teach you.

Personally, I currently have an attorney who charges $1,000 an hour! He's extremely valuable to me. But for every fifteen-minute discussion, it costs me $250! So you better believe that I skip the discussions about the weather and how the kids are doing, and I dive right into the strategic part of my question or need. I do my homework before getting on a call with him. I'm also very conscientious about keeping our calls to fifteen or thirty minutes at most. Most lawyers will simply round up to the next billing block, so someone who bills in fifteen-minute increments will charge thirty minutes for a twenty-two-minute conversation.

In this chapter, I've put together a list of the best and easiest ways I believe you can save money on lawyers. I've organized the list from free to least expensive to most expensive. I hope my legal colleagues don't get upset with me for revealing these strategies. And even if they do, I don't care. There's a reason why I'm affectionately referred to as the "anti-lawyer."

Initial Consultations (Free)

Many lawyers offer free or low-cost initial consultations. This is a chance to understand the legal issue and get a sense of the lawyer's expertise before committing further. We do this at our firm, Premier Law Group. For those who are looking to raise capital, an attorney will sit with the potential new client for anywhere from fifteen to thirty minutes for free—a 100 percent gratuity at absolutely no cost. Our hope is that after we answer legal questions and show our core competency in real estate syndications, the prospect will hire us.

My personal asset protection attorney does the same thing. He once told me that for every ten free consultations he provides, maybe only one will engage him. But it's an expensive engagement, so the free consultations are worth it for him.

Now beware. Not all initial consultations provide free advice. I was once looking for an attorney to assist me and a client with information on how to best structure a project my client was working on. The attorney was very clear that the information he had was valuable, and that he didn't give that away for free, and that we'd need to engage him before he'd give us even an idea of strategy. We ultimately didn't hire him because of that scarcity mentality. Most attorneys are like me. They're happy to give you some free basic legal advice in the hopes that their good will and evidence of expertise will entice you to hire them.

Scarcity Mentality vs. Abundance Mentality

"Scarcity mentality" refers to a belief or perception that there's never enough of something, whether it's money, food, time, resources, or other essentials. Individuals with a "scarcity mentality" tend to see the world in terms of limitations rather than possibilities. This can lead them to make decisions based on fear, hold onto things unnecessarily, or avoid taking risks.

The opposite of this is often called an "abundance mentality" or "abundance mindset," in which an individual believes there's enough for everyone and they can create or find more of what they need or want.

For example, in my practice—unlike the attorney referenced above—I provide free comprehensive consultations, knowing full well that the person I'm talking to will take that valuable information and either do it themselves or hire someone else to do it with my information. I still do it because I know that there are enough clients for everyone and, by helping people, enough of them will eventually hire me to assist them with their needs.

Legal Aid (Free)

For those with limited financial resources, there are numerous legal aid societies that offer free legal services. You generally have to qualify as low income, but not always. Take Legal Services Corporation (LSC), for example. LSC is an independent nonprofit established by Congress in 1974 to provide financial support for civil legal aid to low-income Americans. The corporation currently provides funding to 131 independent nonprofit legal aid organizations in every state, the District of Columbia, and US territories.

There are also legal aid offices (also called legal aid services) throughout the United States. These organizations give free legal advice to people who can't pay for a lawyer. Even though some of these offices mainly help those with very low incomes, others are a bit more flexible with who they help. Many of these offices also have tools and resources that can guide you if you're trying to figure out a legal problem on your own.

According to LawHelp.org, these offices typically assist in areas of domestic violence, family law, housing (such as evictions), and public benefits. In addition, some legal aid offices might help with problems related to immigration, buying things, or disabilities.

Pro Bono Services (Free)

While legal aid societies focus on delivering institutionalized support, many private attorneys contribute to the cause by taking on pro bono cases, which means they offer their legal services "for the public good" without charging their clients. This isn't merely out of the goodness of their hearts; there's a professional encouragement involved. Many legal associations around the world encourage or even mandate their members to dedicate a certain number of hours annually to pro bono work. This commitment underscores the legal profession's recognition of its broader responsibility to society.

Law schools are also a great resource to look at for pro bono help. As part of their curriculum, law students often must satisfy a certain number of hours helping the less fortunate under the supervision of their legal instructor. For a directory of law schools who have pro bono offers, check out the American Bar Association's website.[8]

Speaking of the American Bar Association—the largest lawyer organization in the United States—they have a service through which you can ask a question and a volunteer lawyer will e-mail you an answer for free. You can find their website in the list of free legal resources in the sidebar.

··

Free Legal Resources

This is not an endorsement of any legal service, just a list of some of the legal resources I've seen over the years.

- ✓ **Legal Services Corporation:** https://www.lsc.gov/about-lsc/what-legal-aid/i-need-legal-help.

- ✓ **LawHelp: Allows you to select the state where you live to find out who in your state may be able to help with your legal problem.** https://www.lawhelp.org.

- ✓ **LawHelp Interactive: A website that helps you fill out legal documents for free.** https://lawhelpinteractive.org.

- ✓ **American Bar Association: Lets you ask questions online and have a lawyer answer them. They won't answer questions involving crimes.** https://abafreelegalanswers.org.

- ✓ **Directory of Law School Public Interest & Pro Bono Programs: Find a law school pro bono program in your state.** https://www.americanbar.org/groups/center-pro-bono/resources/directory_of_law_school_public_interest_pro_bono_programs/.

- ✓ **List of Pro Bono Legal Service Providers from the US Department of Justice:** https://www.justice.gov/eoir/list-pro-bono-legal-service-providers.

··

Small Claims Court (Free)

Although small claims courts are free from legal fees because lawyers aren't allowed to represent either party, they're more of a do-it-yourself option. The most you can collect or lose in small claims is relatively minor, ranging on average from about $5,000 to $10,000, depending on your state. Arizona is on the low-end of the spectrum at $3,500, with Delaware and Tennessee on the high end at $25,000. Nolo Press has a great resource that lists each state's small claims court limits.[9]

The small claims process is extremely simple. If you're the one initiating the lawsuit, you simply fill out a complaint that's mostly a check-the-box form letting the court know the nature of the dispute. You're allowed to submit additional documents explaining your grievance with the other person (known as the defendant). The defendant generally has about thrity days to respond, then a face-to-face with the judge can happen in as quickly as thirty to sixty days after the defendant has filed a response.

There's no discovery, so no depositions or pre-interviewing the parties, witnesses, or experts, and no requesting documents. You simply show up to court and present your case. You're allowed to bring witnesses in case the judge would like to hear from them.

I've counseled many people through the small claims process here in California and the best piece of advice I can give you here is simple: try to resolve the dispute amicably by sending demand letters and correspondences to the person you believe owes you money. The key, though, is to write those letters not for the defendant, but for the judge whom you ultimately will be in front of arguing your case. If you can settle without going to court, great. But even if you can't, the goal is to show up to your meeting with the judge and show the court that you did everything in your power not to end up there, as evidenced by all the polite letters and documents you sent the defendant. Remember, the letters, e-mails, and documents you send the defendant are really meant for the judge. The person referred to as "Your Honor" is your audience.

After presenting everything you have to the judge (including potential witnesses), the judge will make a decision fairly quickly, if not on the spot.

Be Prepared (Cheaper)

We discussed this briefly in the introduction, but it's worth digging in a little further. If you want to save the most money here, before meeting with your lawyer, have all the relevant documents organized and a clear list of questions written out. Familiarize yourself with basic legal concepts related to your issue. Keep the chitchat to a minimum and get straight to business.

One way you can avoid this is to negotiate a flat fee. After explaining to the attorney what type of service you need during your initial free legal consultation, try to negotiate a flat fee. This way, you don't have to worry about spending extra time on the phone and you have a little more latitude to use the attorney as an educator. After all, it won't cost you more. Just make sure the flat fee doesn't limit you to a certain number of hours. If it does, you're back to making sure you're well prepared.

Prepaid Legal Plans (Cheaper)

Some companies offer prepaid legal service plans that cover consultation and services up to a certain number of hours. This is one of my favorite ways to save money with attorneys, but it's not for the reason you think. On the front end, it's debatable whether this will save you money, since you're paying normal prices and you may end up not using the service.

However, the savings here come on the back end. It's the old adage that "an ounce of prevention is worth a pound of cure," famously uttered by Benjamin Franklin. When you spend a little money up front, you're more likely to use an attorney to review your contracts, create those entities, or generally check to make sure what you're doing is maximizing your protection if something goes wrong. You end up saving thousands, tens of thousands, and sometimes hundreds of thousands of dollars in future legal fees and/or judgments by making sure all your t's are crossed and your i's are dotted on the front end.

A great way to use prepaid legal services is to get certain documents prepared by less expensive online legal platforms (discussed below), then bringing those documents to your prepaid legal time to review them. This should significantly reduce the expense of drafting those documents.

And whenever you need to constantly update your documents, whether they be independent contractor agreements or even periodically updating your will and living trust, these deposits of prevention can save you tens of thousands of dollars in averted legal disputes thanks to airtight, clear contracts.

Use Paralegals (Cheaper)

When seeking legal assistance, you and your business may be deterred by the potential high costs associated with retaining an attorney. There's a cost-effective alternative, however, that can handle many of the routine tasks traditionally performed by lawyers. This is where paralegals come into the picture.

Paralegals charge a fraction of what an attorney would charge on many tasks, such as document preparation or even drafting wills and living trusts. Thanks to the internet, it's very easy to find virtual paralegals who can perform these tasks. Ideally, I'd still prefer to have an attorney negotiate and draft my legal documents. However, if the decision is between having a professional draft something or not, I highly recommend using a professional, such as a paralegal, because they typically have templates that have been drafted and approved by attorneys.

So what does a paralegal actually do and how do they differ from attorneys? Paralegals, sometimes called *legal assistants*, are trained professionals who perform a variety of legal tasks under the supervision of an attorney. Their extensive training allows them to draft documents, conduct legal research, maintain files, and handle other administrative duties that lawyers often manage. This is why if you're going to use a paralegal, make sure the company you're researching or the individual paralegal has an attorney on staff who oversees them. If not, most paralegals will let you know that they can only assist attorneys.

 PRO TIP

While paralegals are a great resource, it's essential to understand their limitations. They can't provide legal advice, represent clients in court, or perform any tasks that constitute practicing law. Always ensure that a supervising attorney reviews their work, especially for critical documents or significant decisions.

Many legal processes, such as forming a business or filing for a divorce, require specific paperwork. Paralegals have the skills and training to draft many of these documents, ensuring they comply with local laws and regulations. And even when it comes to drafting more important documents, such as wills and living trusts, if the cost of preparation is hanging you up or is cost prohibitive and is preventing you from getting the documents done, having a paralegal draft the documents versus not drafting them at all is an option you should consider.

Online Legal Services

The digital age has ushered in numerous platforms that offer affordable legal solutions. By using these online services, individuals and businesses can significantly save on traditional lawyer fees. Here's how these platforms can be beneficial:

Standard Legal Documents. For straightforward needs such as wills, living trusts, and basic contracts, online platforms provide standardized templates. These templates are often created with input from legal professionals, ensuring they cover essential elements.

Fixed Pricing. Unlike the often nebulous hourly billing of traditional law firms, online legal services typically operate with clear, up-front pricing. This transparency allows users to know the exact cost beforehand, aiding in budget management.

User-Friendly Interface. Designed for the average user, online platforms walk clients through the process using simple language and step-by-step guides. This demystifies the often intimidating legal jargon and processes.

Speed and Convenience. Online platforms are accessible 24/7, allowing users to draft and review documents at their own pace. This convenience eliminates the need for scheduling meetings or phone calls during traditional business hours.

Continuous Updates. As laws and regulations evolve, these platforms frequently update their templates and resources, ensuring that users receive current and compliant information.

WARNING

While online legal services offer many benefits, they aren't suitable for all situations. Complex legal scenarios, negotiations, or specialized areas of law might still require the expertise of a traditional attorney. It's crucial to assess the intricacy of your legal issue. I recommend using the online platform for preliminary work, then consulting a lawyer from your prepaid legal service for final review or specialized advice.

Negotiate Rates (More Expensive)

Engaging with an attorney can be an expensive affair, but it doesn't always have to break the bank. One way I see people throwing away money with lawyers is by not negotiating discounts on the hourly or flat-fee rate. Many attorneys, especially the solo practitioners, go through ebbs and flows in their practice. When they're busy, they tend to raise their rates or refuse to negotiate rates. But if they're slow, it's very common for attorneys to strike deals on a project-by-project basis. By tactfully negotiating lawyer rates, you can access top-tier legal advice without incurring exorbitant costs.

For example, if you're spending $200 an hour on an attorney who would've done the same work for $175, you're literally throwing your money away. Don't hesitate to at least ask or compare rates.

In conclusion, while the expertise of a lawyer is invaluable, it doesn't mean you can't negotiate. Approach the conversation prepared and open-minded, and you might find that quality legal representation is more affordable than you initially thought.

Strategies for Negotiating Rates

Here are some strategies to guide you through the process of negotiating rates:

Do Your Research. *Before accepting rates, research typical rates for attorneys in your area who specialize in the relevant field. Knowing the market rate for the service will empower you and allow you to negotiate confidently and effectively. Remember to account for experience, though, because with experience comes higher legal fees.*

Offer Up-front Payments. *Some lawyers might be willing to lower their rates if you can offer a substantial payment up-front. This provides them with immediate cash flow and reduces their administrative tasks associated with billing. This is particularly effective if they're experiencing a slow season in their practice and need the cash today. Remember, lawyers need to meet payroll, too.*

Bundle Services. *If you anticipate multiple legal needs, discuss a package rate. Bundling services might get you a discount compared to paying for each service separately.*

Discuss Alternative Billing Models. *Instead of traditional hourly billing, consider discussing a fixed fee for the entire project or a contingency fee, especially in litigation cases in which payment is based on the outcome. You may also be able to barter with the attorney, especially if you have a product or service that they need, such as web design, graphic design, marketing, etc.*

Leverage Long-Term Relationships. *If you foresee a long-term relationship or recurring need for legal services, highlight this during negotiations. The promise of steady business might encourage a lawyer to offer a more favorable rate.*

Be Honest About Your Budget. *Transparently discuss your budget constraints. While top lawyers might have less flexibility, those building their practice or with fewer overheads might be more accommodating.*

··

Hire a Specialist

Specialists are more expensive than generalists so this strategy is a little counterintuitive. But hear me out. Law practices are similar to the medical field in which you have a general practitioner that you regularly see as your primary care physician, but there are also specialists such as cardiologists, ob-gyns, or orthopedists. Attorneys are similar and the specialized attorneys charge more than the generalists.

However, in some instances it's important not to focus so much on the hourly rate, but rather on the overall project. For example, it may sound as though the attorney charging $100 an hour is cheaper than the attorney charging $500 an hour, but if the attorney charging $100 needs to spend three hours researching your inquiry and one hour discussing it with you, you've just spent $400. On the other hand, the specialist who charges $500 likely already has the answer based on their experience and may be able to deliver it to you in a thirty-minute phone call, costing you only $250.

STRATEGY

Ask the attorney for an estimated budget. It's not uncommon for attorneys to ballpark what the entire matter will ultimately cost you. They'll generally provide a wide range, but this will help you budget for how much the entire project will cost you.

Avoid or Minimize Litigation

Nothing is more expensive than litigation, especially once you get to a trial. Legal fees often get into the hundreds of thousands of dollars, if not seven figures. The old adage that only the attorneys win in litigation isn't far off.

If you're unable to avoid litigation altogether by settling legal disputes before a lawsuit is filed, at the very least work hard toward some alternative dispute resolution strategies. The primary options are mediation and arbitration, both of which are considerably cheaper than full-blown litigation and trial.

As a former litigation attorney, I can tell you that mediation was always the cheapest way to end a lawsuit and it can sometimes be employed before a lawsuit is filed. If your goal is to minimize legal fees, mediation is a route I highly recommend—so much so, in fact, that I encourage *all* my clients to include a mediation clause in every contract. This clause forces everyone to engage in good faith mediation prior to filing a lawsuit.

What's great about mediation is that an intermediary is selected (called the *mediator*) who's typically an expert in the area in dispute. A great mediator will listen to both sides, then systematically tell each side the weakness in their case and how taking this matter to trial is a crapshoot at best and expensive for certain. Hearing the weaknesses in your position from an independent mediator who you (or really, your attorney) respect is incredibly powerful.

If mediation doesn't work, arbitrating a case instead of going to trial is also a way to save legal fees. In the securities litigation world (where I started my career), all matters were handled in arbitrations. Arbitrations tended to be much faster than going to court, and the streamlined and more informal discovery process results in quicker and less expensive outcomes.

Conclusion

Wasting money is never fun. But wasting money on lawyers is the worst. By staying informed, using available tools and resources, and actively participating in the legal process, you can optimize legal expenditures and not hand over more money to lawyers than you absolutely have to. Remember, it's not about forgoing legal counsel; it's about harnessing it wisely.

5

YOU DON'T NEED MONEY OR CREDIT TO BUY ASSETS AND BECOME FINANCIALLY FREE

One of the biggest misconceptions about investing or starting a business is that you need to use your own money. This chapter focuses on the strategy of using OPM—other people's money. As a securities attorney by trade, my law firm spends 100 percent of its time dealing with clients who use OPM. Later in this chapter, we'll discuss some of the regulations that you need to be aware of before you start using friends, families, and acquaintances to pool OPM. But there are several strategies you can employ today to get started in investing or business that literally requires no up-front capital.

Take my friend Ryan. Before he became an incredibly successful entrepreneur and investor, Ryan used a unique strategy to purchase his first investment property by maxing out $50,000 on his credit cards and using it to fix and flip a small house. Ryan leveraged balance transfers, which allowed him to write a check from his credit card and deposit it directly into his bank account. Instead of using the money to pay off another card balance, he used it to purchase his first property.

Armed with this cash from the credit card company, Ryan generated a profit that allowed him to pay back the credit card and pocket a profit of $20,000 with his flip. This venture not only made him cash positive but also showcased the power of using OPM. In this case, the credit card company was the other person.

Using your credit cards is not the only way to get started. My friend Pace is the foremost expert on creative finance, so he's able to acquire assets with no money and no credit. Thousands of people, for example, acquire assets every day without using their credit. Popular techniques include partnering with someone who has great credit or using seller financing, in which the seller of the asset agrees to carry back some or all of the purchase price in exchange for payments.

Banks are avoided, thus bypassing the need for credit checks and/or requirements. The cash flow from the property pays for the recurring interest expense and any other funds required are borrowed from willing lenders or even your credit cards, as illustrated by Ryan's example above. This benefits the seller by expanding the pool of potential buyers and helping the seller get the price they really want for the asset that they may not be able to get with traditional financing or all cash.

Another method is taking over other people's mortgages. You can buy property, "subject to" the existing mortgage, thereby bypassing the need for credit. Pace is renowned for this strategy and built an entire community around it. Buying a property subject to its existing financing means the loan remains in the seller's name, but the buyer takes title and control of the property and the payments. Any other funds needed to acquire the property, which often include paying all the arrears of the current mortgage holder, are often financed.

You see, many sellers would rather hand the property over to you than to the bank, because a bank will affect their credit. With your help, sellers can get caught up in their past-due payments and walk away from the property without a foreclosure on their record.

You have to think outside the box you may have been exposed to while growing up and while spending time with your peers. But as someone who's involved in this world of OPM, I see these strategies

employed daily. Here are several other methods of acquiring assets
without using your own funds:

Loans: Whether private money loans, hard money loans, or credit
card loans, these often don't require the use of your credit. Hard
money loans are short-term loans from private investors with interest rates that are higher than on conventional loans. They're often
used for real estate investments based more on the property's value
than the borrower's creditworthiness. Private loans are similar to
hard money loans, but typically come from someone the borrower
has a personal relationship with—such as friends or family—which
often makes terms more flexible. And of course, we've already talked
about credit card loans.

You can even use conventional lenders if you already own some
property with equity. The equity from your property (primary or
rental property) can be tapped by a conventional refinance loan
or a home equity line of credit. Because these loans are secured by
your property, they often carry lower interest rates than any of the
loans discussed above.

A word of caution. The strategy of leveraging borrowed capital
from the seller or a third-party lender rather than using one's own
savings to fund an investment or start a business amplifies both the
potential gains and potential risks involved in an investment. This
strategy acts like a double-edged sword that can maximize returns
or make losses more severe. So these strategies are just tools, which
you need to learn to use before you implement them.

Here are a few other creative ways to acquire assets without
using all of your capital:

Preselling: Preselling involves selling a product or service before it's
created. I have a lot of clients who sell online courses, for example.
Many will sell the course (usually at a discount) before ever starting the process of creating it. This allows them to confirm proof of

concept that the course is something people are interested in, but also allows them to finance the course with the initial funds received.

With the advent of technology, several crowdfunding platforms have emerged as places for entrepreneurs to presell their products in exchange for early access or other perks and benefits. Popular crowdfunding platforms include Kickstarter, GoFundMe, and Indiegogo.

Equity Sharing: This is a partnership in which one party provides the financing, while the other provides the labor. When the property is sold or refinanced, they split the profits based on a previously agreed-upon percentage. This is different from a joint venture, which is discussed in detail at the end of this chapter.

Bartering: Don't forget good old-fashioned bartering, which is simply the trading of goods or services without the use of money. A website designer might build a website for you, for example, in exchange for your accounting services.

Syndication: At some point, you get to the level where you're pooling other people's money and using your expertise and knowledge to buy a property, start a business, or make an investment. When you pool resources from other people and the returns you provide to those people are generated by your efforts, this is generally referred to as *syndication.*

For example, you want to buy a $500,000 rental property. You get four of your friends to give you $25,000 each for the 20 percent down payment. In exchange for your friends providing the capital, you agree to do all the work, and everyone agrees to split the profits five ways. Let's say you're able to increase the value of the house by 10 percent, so the return on the investment would be $50,000. That's $10,000 for each person. Your capital partners pocket a nice 40 percent overall profit. As for you, however, your return is infinite—since you put none of your own cash into the deal.

PRO TIP

Remember, most successful investors and entrepreneurs have leveraged Other People's Money at some point. It's a proven strategy to scale and succeed!

OPM Legal Compliance

Once you graduate to doing syndications, because there's an expectation of a return for your investors and those returns are generated by *your* efforts, you're legally issuing those people a security and you enter the world of securities compliance. This will require you to seek professional legal help to navigate the complex web of compliance rules.

SELLING SECURITIES

I know it doesn't really make a ton of sense but whenever you take money from other people you have to ask yourself, "Am I selling this person a security, and therefore have to comply with securities laws?"

Wait ... what?

What do securities have to do with any of this? After all, you're just buying a piece of property with a bunch of your friends. Or you're raising some money to expand your business. Why in the world do you need to worry about securities compliance? This is an extremely valid question that really gets new syndicators into compliance trouble.

The reason is that the Securities and Exchange Commission (SEC)—the governmental agency in charge of protecting investors by regulating securities—defines a "security" in an extremely broad way. While most of us think of securities as stocks, bonds, and mutual funds, the SEC goes much broader than that. In fact, the SEC really doesn't care how you take money from investors, whether it's through a loan, making them a partner in your business, or making them a member of your LLC. They don't even care if you offer them a profit sharing agreement or structure your real transaction as tenants-in-common. Both can be classed as securities in the eyes of the SEC.

The SEC doesn't care about the structure. All they care about is whether you're taking money from passive investors where the returns are generated by your efforts. If the answer is "yes," they consider you to be selling them a security. In other words, if you're the active participant who makes all the decisions that generate the profit for the investment, and your investors are passive and just write you a check but aren't involved in the actual investing, then you've given them a security.

Once you understand this and you determine that you're in the business of "selling securities" per the SEC, there are really only three things to consider:

1. Registering your deal with the SEC;
2. Finding an exemption to registration; or
3. It's illegal!

The Securities Test

If you've ever heard of the Howey Test, then what I just told you is the English translation of this Supreme Court case that the SEC uses to determine whether what you're doing involves securities. The actual four-prong test is as follows:

Step 1: Investment of Money: *There must be an investment of money, goods, or services by your investors.*

Step 2: Common Enterprise: *The investment of money is in a common enterprise, typically meaning you're pooling assets from multiple investors.*

Step 3: Expectation of Profit: *The investor expects to earn a return on their investment, not from their own efforts but from those of the promoters or a third party.*

Step 4: Efforts of a Promoter or Third Party: *The profit comes from the efforts of a promoter or a third party. Essentially, the profit is reliant on the efforts of others.*

Registering with the SEC

Your first option is to register with the SEC, and let me tell you, for our general purposes, this is the last thing you want to do. Registering means doing an IPO—an initial public offering—which for practical purposes isn't an option. Not only will it cost you six or seven figures to go through the registration process but, maybe more importantly, it will take more than a year. So think about it, how many people have twelve to eighteen months to wait for SEC approval while they're in a contract on their rental property that they need to raise money for? And who can afford to spend six or seven figures just to get registered? So registration is usually not something that we seriously consider.

Exemptions

This leaves us with the option of finding an exemption to registration. As an SEC attorney, this is where I spend all my time these days—trying to figure out what exemption my clients should rely on to avoid registration.

No matter which exemption we select, the primary goal of the SEC and state regulators is to ensure investor protection. As such, what the SEC is primally concerned about is ensuring that you're disclosing all the important facts about the investment or not leaving out any that would make some of your statements about the investment misleading or untrue. The details and levels of disclosures will generally depend on which exemption you select and the type of investor you're taking money from.

The good news for us is that even though there are numerous exemptions available to us, there are two that are hands down the most popular exemptions out there. In fact, according to the SEC, approximately 93 percent of all exemptions used consist of these two. The reasons are twofold. First, they're what we call "safe harbors," which means if we comply with the elements of the rule, we're assured of compliance. Capital raisers and their attorneys are always fans of certainty. No guesswork. No relying on a jury panel to determine our fate. If we comply with the elements, we comply with the rule.

The second reason for their popularity is they preempt state laws. This is just a fancy way of saying we generally don't have to worry about the state securities laws of wherever all your investors are located, other than the anti-fraud provisions, which we'll discuss below. Imagine having investors from four different states. You'd need to incur the time and expense of not only hiring a state securities attorney in each of those four states, but also ensuring that the structure of your deal was compliant in all four states as well as the federal law that the SEC is overseeing. That's just a nightmare. So whenever possible, we want to rely on an exemption that preempts the states.

We'll also discuss a third exemption that has become increasingly popular over the years, given some updates to the laws.

RULE 506(B)

By far, the most popular exemption that the industry uses is Rule 506(b), which is part of Regulation D issued by the SEC. More than 90 percent of all investors choose this exemption over its counterpart, 506(c), which will be discussed in the next section.

Why do most choose 506(b)?

Primarily due to its flexibility in being able to accept a limited number of *nonaccredited* investors and not having to verify any investor's accreditation status as you would with 506(c). An accredited investor is generally one who has more than $1 million of net worth, excluding their primary residence, or has earned $200,000 in the past two years with a reasonable expectation of earning at least that much in the current year. When combining incomes with spouses (or spouse equivalents), that threshold increases to $300,000. You can also automatically qualify as an accredited investor if you have certain licenses involving investment advisers. For example, if you have a valid Series 7, 65, or 82 license and are registered in good standing with your state, you qualify as an accredited investor, regardless of your financial situation.

PRO TIP

Know your audience. Before trying to sell your investment to investors, understand the distinction between accredited and nonaccredited investors. It will determine which type of exemption to registration you can rely on!

By using Rule 506(b), you can raise an unlimited about of money and accept up to thrity-five nonaccredited investors, as long as they're sophisticated. You must also file a form with the SEC letting them know what you're doing. It's just basic information about your capital raise, such as who you are, how much you're raising, if you're taking money from nonaccredited investors, which exemption you're relying on, and what your compensation will be, among other things. A copy of that form also needs to be provided to all the states where you have investors.

DEFINITION

Are you a sophisticated investor? To qualify, you'll need to have sufficient knowledge and experience in financial and business matters to make you capable of evaluating the merits and risks of the particular investment.

There are some important limitations of Rule 506(b). Most prominent is the prohibiting of general solicitation and advertising. This exemption is supposed to be a private offering, which means they're meant for friends and family and people you generally have a substantive relationship with. (For how to go about establishing a substantive relationship, I recommend checking out Chapter 4 of my e-book, *The 5 Things Every Syndicator Must Know to Stay Out of Jail*, which you can obtain by going to www.LegalStrategiesForEveryone .com/Substantive_Relationships.) This isn't something that you can openly advertise, post on social media, market on podcasts, or use to solicit investors that you meet at a seminar or online event. There are also some individuals who aren't eligible for this exemption because they're considered by the SEC to be "bad actors," meaning they've previously been involved with some disciplinary actions involving selling securities.

RULE 506(C)

Rule 506(c) is very similar to Rule 506(b), except for two main components. Under 506(c), you're allowed to generally solicit and advertise, and thus you aren't required to have a preexisting, substantive relationship with your investors. You are, however, limited to accepting only accredited investors and you must take reasonable steps to verify that the investors *are* accredited before accepting them into your deal. You can't just rely on their representation or a reasonable belief that they're accredited. Other than these two very significant differences, the remaining elements are the same as 506(b).

506(b)	506(c)
- Unlimited capital raise	- Unlimited capital raise
- No advertising or general solicitation	- General solicitation allowed
- Up to thrity-five nonaccredited investors	- Accredited investors only
- Check-the-box verification	- Reasonable steps to verify accreditation
- No bad actors	- No bad actors
- Preempts state law	- Preempts state law
- Notice filing (Form D)	- Notice filing (Form D)

It's Illegal!

I think it goes without saying (even though I just did) that we don't want to do anything illegal, so we'll skip this analysis for now.

Reg A+

Reg A+ is an informal term used for a Regulation A, Tier 2 offering. Reg A+ has the unique ability to allow you to advertise your offering (similar to Rule 506(c)) but also accept nonaccredited investors (subject to some important limitations discussed below). It's like having your cake and eating it, too. But before you get too excited about this exemption, there are some limitations that may make you change your mind.

As I briefly mentioned before, prior to the update of 2015, no one used Regulation A.

Why?

Because it was increasingly compliance heavy and costly, yet you were limited to raising only $50 million. In addition, Regulation A didn't preempt state law, so investors had to hire an attorney in all the states where they were offering the deal and make sure the offering complied with all those state laws. But two important updates made this exemption more attractive to many investors. First, it raised the limits from $50 million to $75 million. And the SEC preempted the exemption from state law.

With those two changes, Regulation A has become a more popular exemption, especially given the fact that you can advertise, solicit the general public, and take nonaccredited investors.

Now here are some of the drawbacks you must be aware of before you get too excited about advertising to nonaccredited investors. First, this exemption requires SEC approval. It's not quite a full-blown registration but it's often referred to as a "mini-IPO" because you must provide all your offering materials to the SEC and get the offering approved before you can use it. This process typically takes about six to nine months and involves going back-and-forth with the SEC lawyers. This raises the cost of doing a Regulation A to about five or six times what other exemptions would cost. Due to this time frame, it also doesn't really work for real estate investors who raise capital for larger real estate deals because their contracts require them to close on the transaction within sixty to ninety days.

In addition, although the reporting requirements are not as strict as the public companies, Regulation A users must file all kinds of compliance reports, such as annual reports, semi-annual reports, exit reports, and reports every time there's a significant change in the deal. Your financial statements must also be regularly provided, be up to date in the public records, and must be audited.

There's a limit of 500 nonaccredited investors who are able to join your Regulation A offering, which is usually not an issue. However, the limitation for nonaccredited investors is related to how much they can invest. They're limited to 10 percent of either their net worth or annual income, whichever is greater. This is one of the reasons you see a lot of investors in Regulation A offerings with small or nominal amounts such as $500 or $1,000.

In the realm of real estate, Regulation A is a great option for funds that haven't yet identified any properties, since there are no deadlines to worry about. And if a business needs some additional capital and can afford to wait the requisite time and the compliance cost still makes it desirable, Regulation A is something you should definitely look at. For most, the Regulation D exemptions are significantly more attractive.

Disclose, Disclose, Disclose

When it comes to complying with the rules and regulations surrounding raising money from passive investors, the name of the game is *disclosure*. This is done through a document called a *private placement memorandum* (PPM). This is where you generally must disclose to your investors all the ways that your deal could go south and they could lose their money.

Think of the PPM like the medical consent form you're provided with prior to surgery—no matter how serious or minor the surgery is. I always give the example of my oral surgeon. I have terrible teeth and I'm often in need of oral surgery to fix serious problems with them. Even though I'm only "going under" with anesthesia for less than five minutes, I always get that yellow sheet of paper called the medical consent form that tells me all the ways my oral surgery can go wrong, even though I'm simply getting a tooth pulled. I could experience some bleeding, swelling, or infection. I could die!

When I sign the medical consent form, the doctor also signs, and they proceed with the surgery. This is what a PPM does. It provides your prospective investor with all the material information they need to make an intelligent decision as to whether this is a suitable investment for them and their family. You disclose all your conflicts of interest, all the skeletons in your closet, and all the assumptions that underpin your investment thesis and projections. After reviewing, they sign to consent to all the information provided, you countersign, and the investment is complete.

WARNING

Although all material disclosures are important, regulators tend to pay particular attention to the compensation disclosure that you'll directly or indirectly receive. So if you're getting paid as the real estate broker as well, that's fine. Just make sure you disclose this to your investors. If your spouse is getting a benefit somehow, that's OK, too. Just disclose it. When it comes to compensation, I recommend over disclosing just to be safe.

Joint Ventures

A cautious word about joint ventures. A joint venture occurs when two or more parties come together to pool their resources for a particular project or investment, splitting costs, profits, and losses. Many people mistakenly believe that doing a joint venture is not a security. The reality is that you don't get to make that decision. Whether your deal structure is a joint venture or a securities offering will be dictated by the facts themselves—in other words, how you structure your deal. If you have any passive investors for which the returns to that investor were generated by the efforts of a person or group of people other than the investor themselves, it's a security.

STRATEGY

A joint venture isn't inherently a security. Ensure that all participants contribute to returns and are active in the venture to avoid triggering SEC compliance.

This means that for your deal to be considered a legitimate joint venture, all the people involved need to be contributing to the return. You can't have anyone be passive. This generally means that everyone in the deal needs to be actively involved so the returns are generated by everyone's efforts, not just by one person or a few people.

Joint Venture Setup Pointers

If you're trying to legitimately structure your deal as a joint venture and not a security, here are six considerations you should keep in mind:

1. Limit the joint venture participants to a maximum of five people. After that, it becomes increasingly difficult to convince a regulator that everyone is actively involved in the deal.

2. Make sure all joint venture participants have proportionate voting rights. Remember that in order to be considered a joint venture, everyone needs to be active and this accomplishes that.

3. Make sure all joint venture participants can vote on key decision-making functions. (Note: not everyone needs to be part of the day-to-day management team, but everyone should have a real opportunity to use their voting rights.)

4. Don't give yourself unlimited control as manager. The more control you have as manager, the more it looks like a security.

5. In real estate transactions, make sure all the joint venture participants have a vote (via majority) on the hiring and firing of the management team and the property manager, and whether to obtain financing, refinancing (ideally signing on the loan), and selling property.

6. Make sure all the joint venture participants have some sort of experience and skills in a specific business that would provide a benefit to the joint venture.

OPM has become more and more common in today's investment world and it's difficult to find a successful entrepreneur or investor who hasn't leveraged other people's money. Whether used when you're just starting out—like Ryan and Pace did—or when you're looking to scale your business or investments to the next level, using OPM is the way that most successful people I know made their money.

6

DON'T FORGET ABOUT YOUR DIGITAL ASSETS

Slowly but surely, our lives are becoming increasingly intertwined with the online world. From cherished family photos and music collections stored in cloud services to more and more investments in cryptocurrencies and NFTs, our digital footprint grows broader and more complex by the day.

Imagine the pain of losing access to years of memories stored on social media, or the financial loss of an untouched cryptocurrency wallet worth thousands, if not millions, which your loved ones may not even know exists. Digital assets, while intangible, carry both emotional and monetary weight. As our digital interactions increase, there's a pressing need to ensure they're effectively integrated into our estate planning—including asset protection—to ensure that they're not lost in digital oblivion.

Have you ever wondered what happens to all your digital photographs that are on your computer, external hard drive, and in the cloud when you die? What about your photos, posts, and articles on your social media accounts? Surely they just get passed on to your loved ones when you're gone, don't they? And in the age of blockchain, if you have digital wallets that contain cryptocurrencies or NFTs, do your loved ones know where they are and how to access them? Who gets them? And what's the best way to protect them from creditors and litigants?

The realm of digital assets isn't just about safeguarding value; it's about preserving a part of our modern identities. As we delve into the intricacies of planning for digital assets in this chapter, we'll illuminate the pathways to ensuring that your online life receives the same diligent care and consideration as your offline life.

Understanding Digital Assets

Before we dive into some legal strategies and recommendations, we need to have a basic understanding of how digital assets actually exist. Digital assets encompass a variety of assets ranging from social media accounts, e-mails, digital photos, and videos to more tangible financial assets, such as cryptocurrency holdings. So this section is split into two main parts—social media accounts, and the financial and collectible side of things such as cryptocurrencies, NFTs, or anything that's currently being tokenized and housed on blockchain.

SOCIAL MEDIA ACCOUNTS

In today's digital age, our online presence—especially on social media platforms—plays a significant role in our lives. Few people stop to consider, however, that although you might feel you "own" your social media accounts, technically, you're generally just granted a license to use the platform. The content you upload, whether photos, videos, or text, might still be considered yours, but the terms and conditions of the platform could grant the platform specific rights or licenses to use, distribute, or modify your content. Bottom line is the management and transferability of social media accounts, and the content therein, largely depend on the platform's terms and conditions.

The vast majority of social media platforms prohibit the sharing of account passwords, even among family members. Some platforms, such as Facebook, allow for the creation of "memorialized accounts" upon the account holder's passing, but transferring ownership is more complex. The account's assets, such as followers or branding, might be challenging to pass on to heirs in a traditional sense. Think about a YouTube channel that's currently being monetized. Many who have YouTube channels are making thousands, if not millions of dollars. What happens if they die?

Also, be aware that transferring or accessing someone else's account might violate privacy rights or the platform's terms of service. It's crucial to respect these boundaries, even in posthumous situations.

In conclusion, as social media becomes an even more integral part of our identities, it's crucial to understand some of the legal ramifications of owning these accounts. While passing on a social media account isn't as straightforward as bequeathing a physical item (as will be discussed later in this chapter), with careful planning and understanding, it's possible to manage your digital legacy effectively.

BLOCKCHAIN

The new technology of blockchain is particularly important since the vast majority of people have a very poor understanding of how it works. Yet blockchain and tokens will soon dominate our society, like the internet, credit card payment systems, and social media.

Now to be clear, this isn't meant to be a deep dive into this topic, but rather I'll teach you the bare basics so we can understand the estate planning and asset protection concepts discussed later in this chapter. Because if we don't understand the basics, how can we effectively protect these valuable assets and pass them on to our loved ones? For a deeper dive into this topic, I highly recommend digging deep on the internet, where you can become much more educated on the topic than the vast majority of the population. Digital assets aren't going anywhere so, like the internet, you'd better have a basic understanding of them.

Once we understand this basic concept, we begin to appreciate the challenges of trying to secure an asset that we have no direct title to and of transferring those assets upon our death.

HOW DO WE TAKE TITLE TO DIGITAL ASSETS ON BLOCKCHAIN?

Probably the most important concept to understand when it comes to digital assets that reside on blockchain is that you never actually hold title to the asset. Unlike a piece of real estate, cash, stocks, or any other tangible asset, digital assets are simply a line of code that resides on a ledger known as blockchain. So if you "own" a cryptocurrency such as Bitcoin, for example, there's no way for you to actually take title to it. It lives and is held on blockchain, which isn't owned by anyone.

What you actually own is access and control over the digital asset and the ability to move it (i.e., to buy and sell it) or license it to someone else. This access is in the form of "keys" that allow you to unlock the asset and take control of it.

Most people think they hold custody of their Bitcoin, but what they really hold is custody of the keys to access it. These keys are essentially highly encrypted passwords that allow you to lock and unlock your access to the asset and to authorize transactions. There are both public keys and private keys, but we won't go into detail here.

There are three general ways you can hold your digital assets, each requiring a different legal analysis when it comes to protecting them and passing them along to your heirs. First is a custodial wallet that's offered by centralized exchanges (e.g., Coinbase, Binance). If your digital asset is housed on an exchange or an online digital wallet, the exchange acts similarly to a brokerage account such as Fidelity or E*Trade. They hold custody to your keys. But they don't hold title or have custody of the asset itself. The asset itself resides on the blockchain ledger. Since custodial wallets are housed online, they're often referred to as "hot" wallets.

Then there are noncustodial wallets. These are wallets for which you control the private keys directly. These can be online wallets (hot wallets, such as MetaMask and Trust Wallet) or offline wallets housed on physical devices, somewhat similar to USB drives, specifically designed to store cryptocurrency keys. Example of cold storage devices are cold wallets such as Ledger Nano or Trezor). These physical devices only connect to the internet when transactions need to be made, at which point the device signs off on the transaction offline, then transmits the signed transaction online, keeping the actual private keys offline and secure. Again, what your physical device stores are the keys—not the actual asset.

STRATEGY

Hot wallets are convenient for transactions but vulnerable to online threats. Keep only a small portion of your assets in the hot wallet; transfer the majority to a cold wallet when not needed for transactions.

What's Blockchain?

Think of the blockchain as an Excel spreadsheet. Or better yet, a Google Sheet that everyone has access to. The spreadsheet shows how much Bitcoin or other digital assets you own. Every time you send or receive Bitcoin, a new entry is made in this sheet. But here's the twist: everyone can see this sheet and every transaction made, ensuring complete transparency. But before any new entry can be added to the spreadsheet, a majority of people using this sheet have to agree that the transaction is genuine. So, while everyone can view and verify the sheet's contents, no one can make changes to it without the majority's approval. It's a shared ledger in which all transactions are visible but are added only after collective verification, ensuring both transparency and security.

Estate Planning Considerations

While many of us recognize the importance of traditional estate planning—transferring physical property, financial assets, and cherished inheritance items—many overlook the equally significant realm of estate planning for digital assets. This oversight is not just an omission of value, but can also lead to confusion and distress for loved ones during already challenging times.

In Chapter 3, I talked about how I was surprised to see so many documents included in my estate planning binder. Because of those documents, upon my death, my assets and guardianships are handled. And, if I ever become incapacitated, I have medical and financial directives as well.

But what about all my digital assets? How do I legally hold title to them and thus pass them on to my loved ones when I die? Whether you know it or not, if you have an online account, you have a "digital estate." The average American has more than 200 online accounts that require a password, ranging from social media accounts to e-mail accounts, online subscriptions, cloud services, and cryptocurrency or NFT accounts. Does your estate plan have a list of these accounts with the relevant passwords?

The rise of the digital age has ushered in a plethora of new assets that are intangible in the traditional sense, yet hold substantial emotional and financial value. The legal landscape surrounding these digital assets in the realm of estate planning, however, remains a maze that many are trying to navigate. Each digital asset (whether photos, e-mails, online accounts, etc.) has unique challenges when it comes to bequeathing them or ensuring they're managed appropriately after one's death. Unlike physical assets such as houses or vehicles, digital assets often don't have clear titles of ownership, and transferring them after death can become a challenge.

The major challenge arises from the terms of service agreements of digital service providers. Many online platforms, such as Facebook or Google, have specific policies in place for deceased users. These policies often limit or dictate how the account can be accessed or managed after someone's death. In many cases, these terms of service agreements prevent the unauthorized access of accounts, even by heirs or executors, creating potential roadblocks in the estate settlement process.

Furthermore, the legal landscape across jurisdictions varies widely. For example, while some states have enacted the Revised Uniform Fiduciary Access to Digital Assets Act (RUFADAA), which provides clarity on how fiduciaries can access digital assets, many states and countries have yet to address the issue legislatively. This disparity in regulations can lead to confusion, especially if the deceased held digital assets or accounts in multiple jurisdictions.

Cryptocurrencies, another form of digital assets, further complicate the scenario. Their decentralized nature, and the absence of a regulatory body overseeing transactions, make them particularly tricky. If a person passes away without sharing the private key or without providing for its retrieval, the cryptocurrency might remain locked away forever, representing a loss of potentially significant value.

Moreover, with the growing prominence of NFTs in the art and collectibles world, another layer of complexity has been added. NFTs, which are essentially digital certificates of authenticity on the blockchain, can be worth thousands, if not millions, of dollars. Ensuring their safe transfer to heirs requires both technical and legal expertise.

Thus, as the world becomes increasingly digitized, it's essential for the laws to keep pace. A comprehensive understanding of the current legal landscape is imperative for anyone looking to plan their estate in today's digital age. Until a universal standard or comprehensive legislation comes into play, we'll all need to be proactive, taking steps to ensure that our digital assets are accessible and transferable upon our death. While technology has made life more connected and convenient, it has also posed challenges that the legal fraternity and individuals alike must confront head-on.

....

The RUFADAA Road Map

The RUFADAA is a legal framework designed to give fiduciaries clearer access and authority over the digital assets of the individuals they represent, whether due to death, incapacitation, or other reasons. Before its introduction, the murky waters of digital assets often posed significant challenges. Digital assets, which include e-mails, social media accounts, blogs, financial accounts, music libraries, cloud storage, and even cryptocurrency, are governed by terms of service agreements that typically don't account for the rights of fiduciaries. This often led to complications in accessing vital digital accounts and properties during times of crisis or the execution of an estate plan.

But the RUFADAA prioritizes the wishes of the account holder. If a user has directly provided instructions (using online tools provided by the custodian or in a will), those directions are given weight over other directives. If a user hasn't provided explicit instructions, RUFADAA then defers to the terms of service agreement. If that agreement doesn't specify fiduciary rights, the default provisions of RUFADAA will apply.

Fiduciaries can request access to digital assets, but custodians aren't obliged to disclose the contents of electronic communications unless the user explicitly consented or the court orders disclosure.

As of this writing, almost all states have adopted some version of the RUFADAA. Check out www.LegalStrategiesForEveryone.com /RUFADAA for a directory of every state so you can check your own.[10]

....

How to Protect Digital Assets from Litigation

As alluded to above, the main challenge with protecting your digital assets from litigants is the method of holding the assets. Since digital assets that are stored on blockchain are nothing more than a line of code, the question becomes how do you title and hold a computer code?

HOT WALLET STRATEGY

If you hold your digital assets in an online wallet (often referred to as a hot wallet), this means that your wallet is connected to the internet, making it more accessible for transactions but also potentially more vulnerable to online threats such as hacks or phishing attacks.

To protect your digital assets from a potential hack, the key is to maintain only a small portion of your assets in the hot wallet at any given time. The majority should be stored in a cold wallet for added protection, and only the portion that you need to transact should be held in the hot wallet. As soon as your transaction is complete and you don't anticipate needing to transact in the foreseeable future, move your digital assets from the hot wallet to the cold wallet. A sensible strategy to add an additional layer of security is to have multiple keys to authorize a transaction. By distributing these keys to trusted individuals, or storing them in separate secure locations, you reduce the risk of single point failure.

On the other hand, to protect your assets from litigants, the strategy is one that's similar to protecting your brokerage account or bank account. Make sure the online account where you hold your hot wallet is in your LLC and not in your personal name. Coinbase, for example, is the most popular exchange out there and they allow you to open either personal or business accounts. Create a holding LLC and have it own the account.

COLD WALLET STRATEGY

If you want the safest storage available, you should consider using a noncustodial cold hardware wallet for all your long-term digital asset storage. Because cold storage is by definition not online, the wallet is safe from online hackers. Of course, it's susceptible to other security issues such as theft, fire, or loss. Remember, only keep what you plan to use in your hot wallet, and once you're done with your transaction, move your crypto back to the cold wallet.

From an asset protection standpoint, I'd treat the cold wallet (a hardware device) the same way I treat precious metals. Have the device owned by an LLC and, when you transact business, only transact business in exchanges or online platforms where your account belongs to the LLC. I'd also make it a point to record an Internal Revenue Service (IRS) transactional event in the name of the LLC. Sell a small portion of your assets for a capital gain and report that on the appropriate tax form. That's another way to show the world that the asset and keys belong to the LLC, not to you personally.

If you already own a cold wallet that you purchased personally, you could theoretically draft transfer documents in which you transfer the cold wallet from your personal name over to the name of your LLC (similar to gold and silver you've already purchased). Make sure there's a time stamp on that document. So either have a notary sign that transfer agreement or do it through DocuSign.

How to Protect Your Digital Assets

How to secure your digital assets step-by-step:

Step 1: *Create an LLC in one of the top five asset protection states (see Chapter 2).*

Step 2: *Set up a business account in the name of your LLC with the exchange where you plan to purchase the asset.*

Step 3: *Purchase your cold wallet in the name of your LLC. Keep records (receipts, bank statements) showing that the wallet was purchased in the name of the LLC.*

Step 4: *Transfer the asset from the business custodial account to the business cold wallet.*

Step 5: *When possible, have records with the IRS under the name of the LLC. Consider triggering a small capital gain or capital loss so that gain/loss is properly reflected in IRS records.*

DIVERSIFICATION

Avoid the temptation to store all your digital assets in a single wallet or platform, even if it's secure. Diversifying storage methods and platforms ensures that if one avenue is compromised, not all is lost. Wallets, especially hot wallets, are susceptible to hacks. Holding all crypto in one wallet puts the entirety of one's investment at risk, if there's a security breach. By dividing holdings across several wallets, exposure to any single breach is limited.

Diversification also protects you from operational and/or legal risks from the platform. Diversifying across wallets means not being wholly dependent on a single wallet's operational stability. If one wallet service faces downtime or technical glitches, you have access to your other crypto reserves in alternative wallets. And if a wallet platform faces legal or regulatory actions, it might affect your ability to access or use your funds. Diversification ensures that only a portion of your assets would be affected in such scenarios.

Finally, losing access to a cryptocurrency wallet, be it due to lost keys or device failures, can be devastating if it's your sole holding place. Multiple wallets act as a safety net. Even if one wallet becomes inaccessible, you'll still be able to access the rest.

STRATEGY

Implement multi-key authorization for transactions to reduce single point failures. This is similar to having two keys to access a safe deposit box. Distribute your digital keys to trusted individuals or keep them in separate secure locations.

I'll leave you with one last thought and strategy. Until more legal clarity arrives, one of the ways to facilitate the transfer of these digital assets after your death is to have all these accounts in entities, as described in Chapter 1. That way, even after your death, the ownership of digital assets remains the same—in the name of your entity. Any transfers of ownership and control can then be handled at the LLC level.

7

IF YOU HAVE A REAL BUSINESS, YOU MUST HAVE THIS

Every real business, whether big or small, faces risks daily. Businesses that produce a specific product tend to face the risk of lawsuits arising from product defects, insufficient warnings, or other issues that lead to injury or damage. Those that deal with suppliers, customers, or partners face the risk of lawsuits arising from contract disputes. Businesses with physical locations face lawsuits from individuals who get injured on the property due to hazardous conditions. And finally, businesses with employees run the risk of employment-related claims that can arise from current and former employees. Unfortunately, these examples are but a small fraction of the potential risks and lawsuits that business owners face.

We all generally recognize that insurance is a good idea if you own a business. But simply purchasing whatever insurance policy the salesperson (a.k.a. insurance agent) is offering to sell you isn't a wise legal strategy. After all, many agents don't owe you any fiduciary duties and are there to sell you a product. It's more of a hope strategy that if something were to happen to you in the future, you'd be covered.

I've already gone into my pet peeves about insurance coverage and their vulnerabilities (see Chapter 1), but there are some simple legal strategies you can implement to maximize your chances of ending up with coverage in the event of a claim. All of these strategies also apply to your personal insurance so, even if you don't own a business yet or never intend to have one, these six strategies should be applicable to you.

Strategy 1: Understanding Who Your Insurance Agent Is Looking Out For

One of the first things to understand when buying an insurance policy is who the person is who's selling you the product. Are they an independent agent/broker, or are they a captive agent? An independent agent/broker has relationships with several insurance carriers and has the option to shop around for the best policy that fits your particular needs. A captive agent only represents one insurance carrier and is generally considered an extension of that insurance carrier. From a legal standpoint, independent agents/brokers generally have a fiduciary duty toward you to ensure that your interests are placed above the interests of the broker or the insurance carrier. With a captive agent, however, that relationship is much weaker because their primary duty and loyalty typically lies with the insurance company they represent, rather than you.

This isn't to say that captive agents don't have any duties to you, just that they have fewer than an independent broker has. Captive agents still have a duty to provide accurate information to you and not mislead you, as well as a duty to offer you a suitable product. These duties don't rise to the level of fiduciary duties, however, so it's important to understand who you're talking to since your legal remedies may be limited if you're talking to a captive agent.

Strategy 2: Taking the Application Process Seriously

Believe it or not, simply filling out the insurance application is the first place an insurance company can deny or limit your claim. It's the insurance company's first line of defense against having to pay out your claim.

If you fail to disclose relevant or complete information in your insurance application, the insurance company has grounds to deny or severely limit your claim. So make sure you focus, pay attention to the application, and complete it as thoroughly and accurately as possible. Otherwise, you could be looking at an unwelcome insurance denial letter.

Too many of us rush through the completion of the application without taking the time to research and provide complete and accurate information that's requested by the insurance carrier. Misrepresentations—whether intentional or unintentional—can result in severe legal consequences, from voided policies to reduced coverage.

STRATEGY

Most insurance experts recommend that before you fill out any form, you take the time to carefully read through all the questions and instructions. Understand what's being asked of you and gather all the necessary information before proceeding. If you're unsure about a specific detail, it's always better to verify than to guess. Guessing can lead to inaccuracies, which can be interpreted as misrepresentation and result in a voided policy.

So, for example, if you're unsure about the exact date of a previous claim, check your records or contact your previous insurer. If they're asking about past medical visits or procedures, make sure you provide them with all of them, which will necessitate tracking down medical records and making some calls to hospitals and doctors.

Some questions on insurance applications may ask for estimates, such as the approximate mileage you drive each year. Others ask for precise facts. Be clear on which is which and provide accurate data where specific facts are requested.

Be open and truthful about potential risks. For example, if you're applying for home insurance and you run a business from your home, disclose that information. Similarly, for life insurance, if you're involved in high-risk hobbies such as skydiving, it's essential to mention this.

Failure to do so could void your policy and lead to my number-one concern when it comes to insurance policies: making consistent monthly premium payments, then realizing that you're not covered for what you bought the insurance for in the first place.

Avoiding misrepresentation in insurance applications is crucial for maintaining the validity of your coverage and avoiding potential legal complications. By being thorough, honest, and proactive in seeking clarity, you can navigate the insurance application process with confidence and integrity.

Strategy 3: Obtaining Professional Help to Understand Exclusions

One of my biggest pet peeves with the insurance industry is the insane number of exclusions listed on every policy. To a layman or even a noninsurance lawyer, like me, what's actually covered by your policy and what isn't can be extremely complicated and difficult to ascertain. My fear is that many of us are making our premium payments every month, thinking we're covered, only to find out that our incident is excluded from the policy.

This is one of the reasons I typically recommend the prudent strategy of having your insurance policies reviewed by an insurance attorney prior to having the policy issued. Yes, there's a cost, but the ounce of prevention will go a long way toward ensuring that you're getting the coverage that you think you're getting. An insurance lawyer can advise you on what the holes are in the policy and how to plug those holes if you need to, likely in the form of an addendum to the policy that is called a rider.

Strategy 4: Use Umbrella Policies

We discuss umbrella policies in detail below, but the fundamental limitations of most insurance policies are the insurance limits that every policy has. Most individuals, in my opinion, are woefully underinsured and thus an umbrella policy kicks in once your insurance limits are reached.

One of the reasons most people are underinsured is because most policies contain a self-cannibalizing provision that takes out legal fees and costs from the insurance policy. Let's face it. Even if you're in the right, litigation is expensive, especially if you take a case all the way through trial and possibly an appeal. The average cost to take a routine case through trial is between $100,000 and $125,000, and that number only goes up with the complexity of the case. Remember, it isn't just attorney fees—it's also expert witness fees, discovery and investigation costs (including travel), and court costs.

With most insurance policies, you need to deduct these costs from the limits on your insurance. So your $300,000 auto insurance policy can quickly be cut in half after the costs involved in taking the case to trial.

Because umbrella policies act as additional insurance that isn't triggered until your underlying policy is insufficient, premiums on umbrella policies tend to be lower that primary insurance. So they're well worth the strategy of using them.

· ·

Is Your Insurance Policy Payout High Enough?

When buying or reviewing an insurance policy, you must familiarize yourself with the concept of "coverage caps" or "policy limits" and the pivotal role they play in protecting your business assets. Essentially, they denote the maximum payout of an insurance policy during a claim. Businesses (and individuals) face challenges when these caps fall short. Take the instance of having insurance capped at $1 million *and facing a $2 million claim. Such situations expose businesses to financial vulnerabilities, as this means potential depletion of company reserves, securing loans, or going out of business. This is one of the major reasons we discuss layers of asset protection in the first chapter of the book. In the event that your business finds itself staring at a lawsuit or judgment in excess of the policy limits, it's crucial to have a backstop to the insufficiencies of the insurance layer.*

Strategy 5: Periodic Legal Reviews

Similar to estate planning documents, insurance policies should be reviewed periodically to account for personal and business changes, as well as changes in the law. Personal events such as marriage, having children, buying property, or starting additional businesses can not only alter your personal insurance needs, but can also affect your business needs. Laws and regulations related to insurance can also change. Either way, it's wise to review and adjust your policies periodically.

Strategy 6: Understand Your Options

I'm always amazed at the vast array of insurance products that are available for both business and personal protection. Simply being aware of the menu of options can provide you with a strategic advantage when seeking insurance protection. Since every business is unique, each will have unique insurance needs. Let's review some of them.

General Liability Insurance. This common insurance policy provides some general protections against financial loss as a result of bodily injury, property damage, minor medical expenses, libel, slander, and defending lawsuits. It doesn't cover everything, which is why this is a good first insurance to have. However, it must be supplemented with some of the other insurances below.

For example, if a third party (such as a customer) is injured on your business premises or because of your business operations, this insurance can cover their medical expenses and any legal fees if they sue. But it doesn't cover employee injuries or major medical expenses. If your business accidentally damages someone else's property, general liability can cover repair or replacement costs and legal fees. But it won't cover auto accidents and it won't cover damage to your own property (which would be covered under a commercial property insurance policy).

If you're a professional and you make a professional mistake, this insurance policy doesn't cover you because those mistakes are generally covered by an "errors and omissions" policy.

This policy does, however, usually protect against claims such as slander, libel, copyright infringement, and misappropriation of advertising ideas. For instance, if you accidentally used someone else's photo in your ad campaign without permission, this policy would cover you if they sued.

Employment Practices Liability Insurance. If you have employees, general liability insurance doesn't cover them. As a result, employment practices liability insurance (EPLI) has emerged as an essential safeguard for businesses of all sizes. This insurance can protect you from claims made by employees related to issues arising from their employment with you, such as discrimination, wrongful termination, harassment, etc. In a world where a single employment-related lawsuit can cripple your business, EPLI acts as a shield, offering both financial and reputational protection.

As workplace laws evolve and employees' awareness of their rights increases, EPLI is not just good to have, it's a business imperative. Every business aiming for sustainable growth and a positive workplace environment should consider incorporating EPLI into their risk management strategy.

Workers' Compensation Insurance. This insurance provides wage replacement and medical benefits to employees who are injured in the course of employment. In many states, this insurance policy is mandatory.

Property Insurance. Covering damage to business property resulting from a covered peril such as fire or theft, this would be a handy insurance policy to have if you own rental property.

Premises Liability Insurance. This policy protects landlords against legal and medical costs resulting from injuries on their rental property. This is for the classic slip-and-fall incident of a tenant on your property. If the tenant or their guest decides to sue, this policy can help cover legal fees and any potential settlement or award.

Loss of Rents Insurance. Often referred to as Rental Income Protection or Fair Rental Value Coverage, this policy serves as a financial cushion for landlords and property owners. Its primary function is to compensate property owners for the loss of rental income when a rental property becomes uninhabitable due to unforeseen events such as fire, flood, or storm damage. If such incidents result in tenants being unable to occupy and pay rent for the property, this insurance comes into play, replacing the lost income for the property owner.

The duration of this coverage is usually for the time it takes to repair or rebuild the property, ensuring that landlords don't suffer prolonged financial strain. However, it's essential to note that many policies have a predefined time limit. Therefore, understanding the specific terms of the policy is crucial.

Legal Expense Insurance. This is a favorite policy of mine for real estate investors since, generally speaking, tenant lawsuits or demand letters are all but assured in this business. In addition, if a landlord faces legal disputes with a tenant, such as eviction processes or breach of contract issues, this policy helps cover the associated legal fees.

Professional Liability Insurance (Errors and Omissions). This protects professionals against negligence claims due to harm resulting from mistakes or failure to perform.

Product Liability Insurance. For businesses that manufacture, distribute, or sell retail products, this insurance protects against financial loss from a product defect that causes injury or bodily harm.

Commercial Vehicle Insurance. Protecting a company's vehicles and drivers, this insurance can cover a combination of vehicle types and drivers, as well as some types of motorized equipment.

Business Interruption Insurance. Covers the loss of income resulting from a fire or other catastrophe that disrupts business operations.

Home-Based Business Insurance. For businesses operated out of a home, which typically aren't covered by homeowner's insurance policies.

 WARNING

If you run your business out of your home, take extra precaution in reviewing your policy or having an insurance attorney review it for you. If you're not covered, consider buying home-based business insurance.

Key Person Insurance. This insurance is the safety net every business needs for their standout person, who's often—but not always—one of the original founders of the company. They might be the boss, the main product creator, or someone with a unique talent. Identifying these key players is crucial because they're the ones the insurance needs to protect. If the key person can't work, this insurance gives the company money. With this money, the business can keep going strong and doesn't have to panic, even when facing such a big challenge.

With the insurance proceeds, the business can hire replacement talent to give it some breathing room. They can take their time to adjust and plan their next move, and ensure that all other employees still get paid and the lights stay on.

Remember when Apple lost Steve Jobs? It was a big deal. People worried about whether Apple could still be great without him. Fortunately, Apple is a business giant and had plans in place. But for smaller companies that might not have the resources of Apple, losing their key person could mean disaster. That's where key person insurance can be a game changer.

If we dive into the histories of many companies, we'll find tales of businesses that went through hard times because they lost their key person. Some managed to bounce back, while others struggled. The businesses with key person insurance had a safety net—a cushion to soften the blow—and it gave them a fighting chance.

Does your business have a key person? What would happen if that person wasn't able to or no longer wanted to work for the business? Would the business be OK? If not, consider key person insurance.

Personal Whole Life Insurance. Whole life insurance is designed to provide coverage for the entirety of your life. Unlike term insurance, which offers protection for a specified term (e.g., ten, twenty, or thirty years), whole life insurance promises a death benefit that will be paid out to the beneficiaries whenever you pass away— whether that's tomorrow or decades in the future—as long as premiums are paid. In other words, it's a policy that's guaranteed to pay out.

An advantageous feature of the whole life insurance policy is that a portion of the premiums paid goes into a cash-value component, which is like a bank account inside the policy. That portion of the premiums grows over time on a tax-deferred basis, meaning you generally won't pay taxes on the gains unless you withdraw them. The cash value of a whole life insurance policy can be thought of as a savings component. You can borrow against the cash value or surrender the policy that distributed the accumulated cash value. Surrendering, however, terminates the death benefit.

Whole Life Insurance for Businesses. Whole life business insurance works the same way the personal whole life insurance does. The main differences are its purpose and the strategies that we use. Instead of using the cash value of your policy to make personal investments, the cash value of your business whole life insurance can be used for business purposes.

It's important to note that the business is the actual policyholder for the benefit of each business partner. In the event that one of the business partners dies or unexpectedly departs, the business can continue.

On the death side, most business partnership agreements contain a "buy-sell" agreement in which the surviving business partner agrees to buy out the ownership interest of the deceased partner from their estate. That way, the surviving business partner isn't forced to continue in the business with a new partner who may not be desirable. The purchase price of the share in the business now owned by the estate of the deceased partner is often an amount that the surviving business partner can't afford to pay without obtaining a loan or some other financial arrangement. The proceeds from the business whole life insurance policy are thus used by the surviving partner to pay for the interest of the deceased partner.

However, just like the additional benefits of the personal whole life insurance, the benefits of such a policy for business extend far beyond simply handling the deaths of the partners. The liquidity of the policy's cash value can be used to help the business in the event of a sudden departure of a partner or to assist with any temporary funding shortfalls. The cash-value liquidity can also help the business make investments into the future by recruiting additional talent or purchasing equipment that can increase the company's revenues.

STRATEGY

Whole life insurance is not just an insurance policy. It's an asset. Use it for collateral to obtain loans from a bank or third party. This simplifies the loan process and fetches more favorable terms.

Business Umbrella Policies. The world of insurance is vast and intricate, with multiple policy types designed to offer coverage in various situations. Among these are standard policies that are tailored for specific business needs, as discussed above. However, there's an unspoken reality in the insurance sphere: basic insurance policies often come with substantial limitations. To put it simply, these standard policies offer the bare essentials. They're designed to cover the basics, but might fall short when faced with larger, more complex issues. As a result, many businesses will find that the coverage limits of these basic policies can be quickly exhausted in the face of a significant claim or lawsuit. This is why modern businesses need umbrella coverage.

To better grasp this limitation, consider the variety of scenarios that could arise in a business, which range from property damages to cyber threats, and each carries its own set of risks. A basic insurance policy might cap its coverage at a certain amount, let's say $1 million. While that might seem like a substantial amount, the cost of legal battles, settlements, and other associated fees can quickly diminish that amount.

Take the scenario in which you're a business owner, and you believe you've taken all the necessary precautions by insuring your company. One day, an employee decides to sue your company for a work-related injury or perhaps a discrimination issue. The lawsuit goes to trial, and the judgment goes against your firm. The judgment amount? A staggering $2 million. Now, if your existing policy has a coverage limit of $1 million, where does that leave you? After legal fees and the cost of the trial, you might find that your basic insurance has been drained considerably, leaving a massive gap.

This is where an umbrella policy becomes indispensable. Umbrella policies are aptly named; they act as a protective canopy, ensuring that businesses are shielded from the potential financial downpour of overwhelming claims. When a primary policy reaches its limit, the umbrella policy kicks into gear. In our aforementioned scenario with the $2 million lawsuit, the umbrella policy would cover the remaining $1 million plus liability, ensuring that the company doesn't face financial ruin.

There are other benefits to having an umbrella policy, beyond just filling in the gaps. With the ever-evolving landscape of business risks, especially in our digital age of cybersecurity threats, unforeseen challenges arise all the time. An umbrella policy can adapt to cover these new and unexpected risks, offering businesses the flexibility they need in today's fast-paced world.

Furthermore, having an umbrella policy can also boost a company's credibility. Partners, clients, and employees can have added confidence in the stability and responsibility of a business that's well insured. It shows a commitment to ensuring that everyone involved with the company is protected.

In conclusion, while all the basic insurance policies discussed above play a fundamental role in business protection, they're just the starting point. Given the multifaceted risks in today's business world, an umbrella policy is a necessity. It provides that added layer of protection, ensuring that businesses can weather even the most significant financial storms. As the business landscape continues to evolve, it's paramount for companies to stay ahead of the changes, and having comprehensive coverage is an integral part of that journey.

Tail Policies. Some professions have responsibilities that last a long time. They need protection even after they stop working. That's where "tail policies" help. Think of them like an extended warranty for a person's work.

For example, you work as a real estate agent and you facilitated the sale of a rental property last year. Both the buyer and seller were happy, and the deal was sealed. Now, fast forward to a year later, and the buyer claims there's a serious hidden defect in the property and they're pointing a finger at you, wanting to sue you for not disclosing it.

"What?!" you think, "That was a year ago!"

Imagine you owned a plumbing service. A few years ago, you completed a large job installing the plumbing system for a new house. The homeowners were thrilled, you got paid, and you moved on to other projects. Fast forward to now. The homeowners reach out claiming there's a major leak due to your team's installation, and they're thinking of suing for damages.

"But that was years ago!" you think.

You're a professional—a lawyer or a doctor. During your professional career, you carried malpractice insurance but have now decided to retire. You may think you no longer need the malpractice insurance since you're no longer practicing. But what about those lingering cases or patients?

For example, you are an attorney and you draft an asset protection trust for your client. Several years after you retire, your former client gets sued by a plaintiff and the asset protection trust you created didn't work and your former client lost everything. Your former client sues you for malpractice for poorly drafting asset protection documents.

Imagine you are a doctor and you perform surgery on your patient. Everything seems fine at first, but several years later your patient develops complications that are attributable to the surgery. Your former patient sues you for medical malpractice.

You are a real estate investor and hold one of your rental units in an LLC. Your LLC sells the property to a buyer. Years later, mold is discovered in the property that you and your LLC failed to disclose to the buyer, which has created serious health problems for the buyer. The buyer sues the LLC that sold the property for failure to disclose.

These scenarios are where tail policies come into play.

When we talk about tail policies in insurance, we're talking about a special kind of safety net. It's insurance that still works even after you've finished a job, sold a product, or stopped offering a service. It's like making sure you're covered for things from the past that might pop up in the future.

I know insurance is a boring subject, but if you're running or planning to run a real business, this is the cost of doing business in today's ultra-litigious society. While a keen business sense and a solid plan can help you navigate a lot of challenges, there are certain unexpected events which, even if ultimately resolved, can be expensive and time consuming. Insurance provides a safety net, ensuring that a single event doesn't financially devastate your business.

Benefits Beyond Risk Management

Business insurance also provides benefits that go far beyond risk management. For example, it can enhance credibility. Customers and clients find solace in knowing they're dealing with a business that's insured. It conveys a message of trustworthiness and assures them that, if something goes wrong, there's a system in place to provide compensation.

Business insurance can also indirectly protect the most valuable asset of any business—its employees. Insurance can help in providing benefits to employees, safeguarding their health and well-being. It also aids in attracting and retaining talent. Many jurisdictions and industries actually require businesses to carry certain types of insurance. For instance, if you have employees, workers' compensation might be mandatory.

And finally, business insurance provides one of my personal favorites: peace of mind. With the right insurance, business owners can focus on what they do best—running their business—knowing that potential pitfalls are covered. Peace of mind also fosters an environment that's conducive to growth and innovation.

The bottom line is this: if you're genuinely invested in your business and its future, insurance isn't just an option—it's a must-have.

8

IT'S TIME TO BRING OUT "THE WINTER COAT"

As mentioned in Chapter 1, when you consider legal strategies to protect your wealth, it's important to understand that asset protection isn't a single strategy, but rather several layers of strategies or protection. The level of protection you should consider is primarily dependent on where you are in life, how dangerous your career is, and how much you have to protect. If you're young and have nothing to your name except a consistent W-2 paycheck and a small rental unit, maybe insurance is enough. But, if you have millions of dollars to your name, a thriving business, and numerous rental properties, a $1 million insurance policy is obviously not enough.

In Chapter 1, we gave the analogy that layers of strategies are like layers of clothing that you wear depending on how warm or cold it is outside. Well, in this chapter, we discuss how to apply that "winter coat" layer when you have a lot to protect and you're in an environment that makes you much more susceptible to lawsuits.

We'll discuss two advanced strategies: APTs and equity stripping strategies.

....

The 6 Asset Protection Layers

Below is a summary of the asset protection layers outlined in Chapter 1.

Layer 1: *Existing laws that partially protect your assets: homestead exemptions, certain retirement accounts, etc.*

Layer 2: *Insurance policies*

Layer 3: *Privacy*

Layer 4: *Entity Structuring*

Layer 5: *Asset Protection Trusts (APTs)*

Layer 6: *Equity Stripping Strategies in which you remove equity of an asset and place it into a safer entity.*

....

APTs in General

I genuinely believe that if APTs were handed out for free, everyone would have one. So what exactly is an APT?

Structurally speaking, an APT is very similar to a living trust when it comes to the parties involved. Like a living trust, an APT is a separate legal entity that has a settlor/grantor, which is you— the person who creates the APT and designates all the parties. You decide which assets should go into the APT, how it should operate, and for whose benefit it should be managed. Also, like a living trust, the beneficiaries are the individuals or institutions that you designate as the ones who'll receive your assets. While you're alive, you or a designated entity can be the primary beneficiary of the APT. After you die, the assets or income from the APT will be distributed to the designated beneficiaries, which can include family, friends, charities, or other entities. Although the APT also has a trustee like one has in a living trust, in this case, it's usually a third-party trustee based in the state or country where the APT is created. APT trustees should be large institutions that are insured and that manage hundreds of millions of dollars, so your estate is not significant in their world. Otherwise, there is always a risk of the trustee (who has all the control) stealing your funds. So you don't want your Uncle Bob being the trustee or the local cab driver in some foreign jurisdiction. When there is a lot of money involved, the incentive to commit wrongdoing grows exponentially.

Because of the third-party nature of APT trustees, some APTs also designate a "protector" who acts like a veto mechanism to keep the trustee in check. While APT trustees hold legal title to the trust assets, and are responsible for managing and distributing them according to the trust's terms, protectors provide an additional layer of oversight. The role of the protector can vary based on the APT, but they typically have the power to appoint or remove APT trustees, approve or veto certain trustee decisions, and ensure the interests of the trust's beneficiaries are preserved.

 PRO TIP

Including a protector can enhance flexibility, provide checks and balances, and address concerns about APT trustee misconduct or incompetence. Make sure you select someone trustworthy, who has impeccable integrity, and who'll prioritize the best interests of the APT's beneficiaries. If you have someone like that who's also an attorney, that's even better.

Unlike living trusts, however, which have no asset protection qualities whatsoever, an APT provides the strongest asset protection available under the law, which is why it's favored by so many wealthy individuals.

APTs can be either active or dormant. Let's use a basic bank account as a simple example. With an active trust, the bank account would be owned directly by the APT. This means anytime you wanted to move money in or out of your bank account, you'd need to call the APT trustee and make the request, and that trustee would execute the request. This scenario is not ideal. Most commonly, APTs are dormant, which means they're paired with an LLC such that the APT merely owns the LLC and the LLC in turn owns the asset. In this case, the LLC owns the bank account. Because you'd be the manager of the LLC, you're still able to "control" the bank account even though you don't have legal title to it. Remember, *own nothing, control everything.*

Key Benefits of APTs Over Other Entities

The key differences and benefits of an APT over other entities, such as LLCs and corporations, is the superior asset protection quality of trusts. There are several traits of an APT that give it this superior quality.

Trait 1: Complete Removal of Ownership. The key difference between a non-trust entity and an APT is the removal of legal ownership. An APT is a completely separate entity that has no owners, and thus you no longer have any legal ownership to property inside an APT. You merely retain beneficial interests in the APT assets, meaning you get to enjoy the use of the property inside the APT. LLCs, on the other hand, have owners. You either directly own the LLC that owns the asset, or you own an LLC that owns the LLC that owns the asset. Either way, with an LLC, there's an ultimate owner. With an APT, there isn't.

In the US legal system, liability attaches to ownership. So if you legally don't own the asset, no one can take it away from you.

This distinction of ownership is a fundamental difference between APTs and LLCs, and it's the main reason why APTs, in general, are considered superior to all other forms of entities.

Trait 2: Irrevocability. APTs are irrevocable. Once assets are placed in an irrevocable trust, the settlor generally can't unilaterally modify, amend, or terminate the APT or its terms. This lack of control by the original owner further cements the distinction between personal assets and APT assets.

Trait 3: Spendthrift Provisions. A spendthrift clause prevents beneficiaries (i.e., you) from pledging, selling, or assigning their expected APT distributions to others. This protects the APT's assets from creditors by adding another layer of asset protection.

Trait 4: Third-Party Trustee(s). APTs are generally administered by an independent third-party trustee who holds legal title to the APT's assets. This legally removes your ownership, all the way up the ownership track.

Trait 5: Discretionary Distributions. Unlike some trusts, APTs don't have fixed distribution standards, such as distributions for "health, education, maintenance, and support." Instead, they're entirely discretionary, which means creditors can't easily force the trustee to make distributions even if a creditor were to obtain a court order entitling it to the beneficiary's distributions.

Trait 6: Self-Settled Nature. The term *self-settled* refers to the origin of the assets that are placed into the APT. Typically, these assets come directly from one of the potential beneficiaries. In many states, creditors can penetrate such APTs if the grantor or beneficiary has outstanding debts. However, in the states that recognize APTs, this isn't the case—assuming all relevant rules are adhered to.

Legal Ownership vs. Equitable Ownership

*Legal ownership and equitable ownership are foundational concepts in property law. **Legal ownership** refers to the formal, recognized right to property, often recorded in public registries, giving the holder the right to control, transfer, or sell the property. Conversely, **equitable ownership** refers to the beneficial interest or use of the property. While the legal owner holds title and bears responsibilities for the property, the equitable owner enjoys the actual benefits or use of it. This is what happens with trusts, in general. The trustees have legal ownership, ensuring the property is managed according to the trust's terms, while beneficiaries have equitable ownership, enjoying the assets" benefits.*

Let's apply this concept to Bob—the person who injured Skateboarder Sam in our earlier chapters and had a judgment obtained against him. Consider how Bob's assets will be attacked. If Bob owns rental property in an LLC only, without a trust, Skateboarder Sam's attorney will ask the judge to hand over the ownership of the LLC to his client so he can liquidate the property and satisfy his judgment.

Bob tells the judge that the LLC has charging order protection and thus his ownership in this LLC can't be taken. But Bob lives in a state where a charging order is not Skateboarder Sam's exclusive remedy and the judge decides to provide foreclosure relief to him, thus allowing Skateboarder Sam to take ownership of Bob's LLC.

Now consider a trust. The same judgment is obtained against Bob, but he doesn't own the trust so the trust can't be touched. The charging order doesn't even come into play (see Figure 8.1).

Fig. 8.1

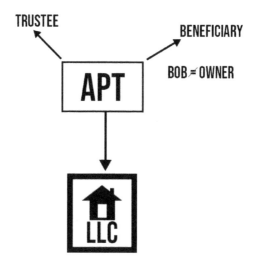

One of the benefits of APTs is also a concern that comes up for some individuals. That concern is the irrevocable nature of the trusts. Meaning once you hand over all your assets to the trust, you can't amend or modify the terms of the trust, which is unsettling for some. However, having the dormant structure referenced above should alleviate some of this concern since the only asset in the trust is an LLC that can own, purchase, or sell whatever assets are underneath it. And you can retain control of the LLC by becoming its manager.

Domestic APTs vs. Offshore APTs

There are two main types of APTs. Some are set up right here in the United States, and others are set up in different countries. Both have their own sets of benefits and things to watch out for. In this chapter, we'll explore domestic and offshore APTs, helping you understand how they work and the pros and cons of each.

DEFINITION

*A revocable living trust **is not** the same as an APT, which is irrevocable. A living trust (discussed in Chapter 3) has no asset protection value whatsoever. Its sole purpose is to avoid probate. An APT, on the other hand, is irrevocable and thus whatever is inside the trust can't be accessed by creditors if structured properly and legally.*

Domestic APTs: As the name implies, domestic APTs (DAPTs) are trusts set up under the laws of a particular state in the United States. Keep in mind, not all states have DAPT laws. As of this writing, the following states have adopted DAPT laws: Alaska, Delaware, Hawaii, Michigan, Mississippi, Missouri, Nevada, New Hampshire, Ohio, Oklahoma, Rhode Island, South Dakota, Tennessee, Utah, Virginia, West Virginia, and Wyoming.

I'm partial to Nevada as being the best state in which to create your DAPT, and usually recommend that clients look there first.

Why?

Nevada is one of the states that has the shortest statute of limitations, which is two years from the date of the transfer to the trust or six months from the time the creditor could've or should've discovered the transfer, whichever is later. This means that typically after two years from the date you transferred your assets into the trust, creditors are generally prohibited from claiming that a fraudulent transfer was made to avoid creditors.

Offshore APTs: An offshore APT (OAPT) is an irrevocable trust created in a jurisdiction outside the United States. Sometimes referred to as an *international asset protection trust*, it's essentially identical in structure to a DAPT except that it's created in an offshore jurisdiction and the trustee is located in that jurisdiction.

The world offers a wide array of choices for establishing an OAPT. Notable jurisdictions include the Cook Islands, Isle of Man, Belize, and Nevis. Each of these jurisdictions has introduced laws that favor the establishment and management of OAPTs. Although the best choice isn't universal, most offshore specialists are partial to the Cook Islands as the gold standard for offshore jurisdiction. This is typically because this small island off the coast of New Zealand was among the first jurisdictions to introduce specific APT legislation in the 1980s. Their trust laws are tailored to the needs of those seeking strong asset protection features. For example, for a creditor to breach the trust assets, they often need to litigate their claim in a Cook Islands court, proving the claim "beyond a reasonable doubt," which is a higher standard than the "preponderance of evidence" standard common in US cases. The Cook Islands also don't recognize foreign judgments and have a very small statute of limitations window.

Some jurisdictions might hold unique advantages over others, depending on your individual needs. Thus, it's vital to engage experts to analyze your specific needs and select the most fitting jurisdiction.

Choosing between domestic and offshore trusts is all about weighing the pros and cons. It's about understanding what's at stake, what you're comfortable with, and where you see the most benefit. There's no right or wrong answer and the best choice varies from person to person.

WARNING

A word of caution. There's often talk about taxes when discussing APTs. Although there are certainly some ways to use a trust as a tool to help you with your tax planning, generally speaking, APTs are tax-neutral, meaning they don't provide any beneficial (or negative) tax treatment. They're primarily to protect your hard-earned wealth.

Advantages of DAPTs

There are three primary advantages that a DAPT has over an OAPT, most of which are really just not having the negatives.

Benefit 1: Cost Effectiveness. Although a DAPT is significantly more expensive than creating a simple domestic LLC, DAPTs offer a significant discount in cost and ongoing fees when compared to their offshore counterparts. Don't be surprised if you have to pay up to three times more for an OAPT.

Benefit 2: No Jurisdictional Risk. Most people are more comfortable operating under the laws of the United States and hiring US managers and advisers, because we're much more familiar with them, and the laws and system aren't subject to the political and other risks inherent in offshore jurisdictions. While many offshore jurisdictions are stable, some individuals may be wary of the political and economic risks in foreign countries. In contrast, the United States is seen as having a stable political and economic environment, which can offer peace of mind to those establishing a trust. Familiar US laws and regulations also lead to a more straightforward management of DAPTs compared to OAPTs.

Benefit 3: Reduced Scrutiny and Compliance Burden. OAPTs often come with rigorous requirements for reporting to US tax authorities, such as the IRS. Failing to comply with these requirements can lead to significant penalties. DAPTs, being domestic, don't have the same level of international reporting complexity. Also, offshore trusts can sometimes be perceived as dubious or as tax-evasion schemes, even if they're legitimate and compliant. Using a DAPT can avoid this stigma because they're US-based and recognized by specific state statutes. Offshore trusts are 100 percent recognized in the United States under the Hague Convention, which was entered into by the United States. So the stigma is really unwarranted but a reality nonetheless.

Disadvantages of DAPTs

The main disadvantage of DAPTs is that they're still within the jurisdiction of the US court system and subject to the jurisdiction of US judges. With an offshore trust, most jurisdictions don't recognize US judgments and thus the actual trust is removed from the reach of courts, directly.

Another disadvantage with DAPTs, and APTs in general, is that most people are a little (or a lot) uncomfortable with the fact that they don't directly control their assets. If we recall how we started this book with "own nothing, control everything," it would appear that you lose both with a trust. Although the institutional trustee will be fully bonded and insured, the easiest way to get comfortable with a trust is to make it dormant, as discussed above. This will ensure you retain control and management.

DAPTs are also not recognized in all states, so if someone from a non-DAPT state tries to claim the assets, the courts may attempt to ignore the trust. While the US Constitution mandates that states should recognize and respect the judgments from other states (the "full faith and credit" clause), the exact interpretation of this as it applies to DAPTs remains unsettled at the highest levels of the judiciary. So, if a DAPT owns real estate in a state that doesn't recognize these trusts, a local court could potentially exert jurisdiction over that property. This jurisdiction could allow the court to bypass the DAPT's protective measures and use the property to satisfy a judgment.

Advantages of OAPTs

The fundamental strength of transferring assets to an OAPT lies in the protective shield it offers. This process effectively removes the assets not only from your legal ownership, but also from the clutches of the US legal system, placing them securely in the chosen jurisdiction. But this doesn't equate to losing control. On the contrary, the assets remain within your grasp, especially when the OAPT is thoughtfully paired with entities such as an LP or LLC.

This strategy imports the benefits of foreign laws without the need to physically transfer assets out of the United States.

Moreover, anyone determined enough to challenge an OAPT is in for a rigorous journey. They'd have to initiate their legal claim in the offshore jurisdiction, which comes with its own set of challenges. The financial and legal hurdles, combined with high standards of proof, often dissuade most from even embarking on this journey.

Disadvantages of Offshore Trusts

Although considered the gold standard of asset protection, OAPTs aren't without their kryptonite. While a US court doesn't have jurisdiction over the foreign trust itself, it does have jurisdiction over individuals present within the United States or under its legal authority.

As a result, if a judge believes that the trust has been used to perpetuate a fraud or doesn't believe that you have no ability to control the trust and/or trustee, the judge can order you to bring those assets back to the United States. If you don't or can't comply, the court can find you in contempt. This can result in various penalties, including fines or even imprisonment until you comply with the order.

Some individuals have attempted to use the "impossible act" defense. They argue that they can't comply with the judge's request to move funds back to the United States because they don't have the control or authority they're believed to have or that the laws of the foreign jurisdiction prevent them from complying. However, success with this defense varies. Courts might argue that the trust was set up to make it appear that the defendant doesn't have control when, in reality, they do.

Look Before You Leap into Offshore Trusts

Probably the most famous case involving individuals being sent to prison for contempt of court is the FTC v. Affordable Media, LLC, *case better known as the "Anderson Case." The Andersons are a husband and wife who were involved in a Ponzi scheme. Following the scheme, the Andersons set up an OAPT to try to hide their ill-gotten gains. The court rejected their argument that it was impossible for them to comply with the court's order to bring back the funds from their offshore accounts. When the Andersons insisted on their position, they were thrown in jail for contempt of court.*

The Anderson Case is a notable example of the risks associated with offshore trusts and the US court's power to coerce compliance through contempt.

In yet another case, Stephan Jay Lawrence created a Nevis-based APT and subsequently transferred substantial assets to it. Later, a judgment was issued against him in a US court. When the creditors tried to collect, Lawrence claimed that he couldn't repatriate the funds because he no longer had control over the trust assets.

The US court ordered him to bring the assets back to the United States to satisfy the judgment. When he didn't comply, claiming he wasn't the trustee and thus had no control over the assets, the judge disagreed and Lawrence was held in contempt of court and incarcerated. He spent more than a year in jail for his noncompliance.

This case serves as a cautionary tale for those considering offshore trusts as part of their asset protection strategy. It's crucial to understand the potential legal risks and to consult with experts who are knowledgeable about domestic and international asset protection laws.

Cost is another impediment to establishing an OAPT. Legal fees to create the trust can range from $25,000 to $50,000, while ongoing trust fees and expenses require a hefty annual maintenance cost.

Finally, there are crucial regulatory and tax compliance mandates. The IRS, for instance, requires that all income generated from the offshore trust be duly reported and taxed every year. Regular and timely compliance, however, not only safeguards against legal repercussions but also adds a layer of legitimacy to the trust. This can be instrumental if ever challenged in a court of law.

Equity Stripping Strategies

Equity stripping strategies are the other advanced asset protection strategy that we want to address in this chapter. Equity stripping involves reducing or eliminating the equity in a property or asset to make it less attractive to creditors.

Below are two ways to accomplish this.

Liens: Imagine you get a home equity line of credit (HELOC) on your house. The bank gives you a credit line of $500,000. Whether you pull money from the HELOC or not, the bank will place a lien on your property to secure the entire line of credit. If you borrow against your line of credit, the equity in your home essentially is removed from your home and handed to you in the form of cash, allowing you to invest, spend, or hold those proceeds. If a judgment was ever obtained against you, the equity in your home wouldn't be available, because there wouldn't be any. There would be a first mortgage by your primary lender encumbering most of the property and the HELOC second lien.

Similarly, for other assets, you can encumber them with loans and have the loans secured with a UCC-1 financing statement. This places a lien on the asset. Similar to a recorded property lien, a UCC-1 filing puts the world on notice that you have a security interest (i.e., a lien) on that asset so in the event the owner of that asset doesn't pay the debt, you are allowed to start legal proceedings to take legal possession of the asset to satisfy your loan. Your rights to take legal possession of the asset will supersede any other person who files a lien (i.e., a UCC-1) after you. You can literally secure anything, including assets inside of your business and accounts receivable.

Now it's true that there's a cost to this strategy—the loan has an interest rate that needs to be paid. The true cost of the strategy is the difference between the interest rate being charged and the risk-free rate of treasuries. As of the writing of this book, you can buy risk-free, short-term treasuries for about 5 percent, and HELOC rates hover around 9 percent. This means that the cost is 4 percent. You'll need to think of this cost as an insurance cost securing the equity in your home.

But what if you can't get a HELOC or a third-party loan to encumber your assets? This lien strategy calls for you to be your own lender by creating your own LLC to act as the lender. Ideally, your lending LLC is owned by your APT. Your lending LLC then loans, or provides, a line of credit to the legal owner of your rental property or personal residence. And, in exchange, your lending LLC places a second lien on the property.

In a perfect world, you document the loan payment from your lending LLC to the legal owner of the asset. If you're unable to pull all the loan proceeds at once, use the line of credit to slowly pull the money out over a longer period of time. Even if you haven't pulled the entire line of credit, the lien will still be placed on the property and any plaintiff's lawyer doing a property or asset search will come across the second lien and see that there's no equity in the home to pursue.

How the Lien Strategy Works

Here's a basic overview of how the lien strategy equity strips your assets:

Step 1: Create an Entity. *Set up an LLC in a strong asset protection state, such as Wyoming, Nevada, or Texas. If you live in one of those states, create it there. Let's call this your "lending LLC." Ideally, this LLC is owned by your APT.*

Step 2: Create Documents. *Have your attorney create the loan documents or line of credit to properly document the transaction.*

Step 3: Transfer Funds. *Have your lending LLC transfer money to the legal owner of your property or assets. If you can't transfer the money all at once, transfer it over time until the entire line of credit is consumed.*

Step 4: Record. *Record the loan and/or line of credit with the appropriate agency, typically the county recorder's office where the real property is located or a UCC-1 filing for personal or business property.*

Step 5: Document. *Keep all these records, including transfer records, in the event you're involved in a lawsuit.*

Figure 8.2 is a visual representation of this strategy.

Fig. 8.2

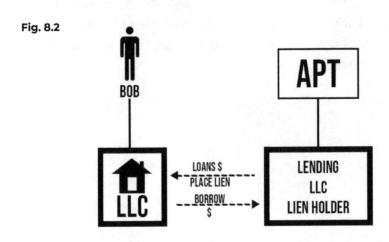

Leases and Licenses: A similar concept is to use leases instead of loans. For example, let's say you own a business that has valuable equipment, or maybe your own the building where the business is conducted. Instead of the business owning the equipment or the building, you could have the equipment or building owned by an LLC you create that does no business with anyone other than leasing the equipment or property to the business. For example, you own a dental practice that has dental equipment worth hundreds of thousands of dollars, as well as the office where the dentists work. Another LLC can purchase and have title to the dental equipment and the building, and enter into a lease agreement with your dental practice. This way, the dental equipment and building would no longer be owned by the dental practice and would be outside the reach of creditors.

Or think of all the intellectual property that your business has. The same LLC could take ownership of the intellectual property (customer lists, domain names, websites, trade secrets, processes, and systems) and simply lease or license the intellectual property back to the business. You can literally strip the ownership of everything inside the business and place it into a safe LLC that's unrelated to the business.

In all these examples, the business not only doesn't own the assets but they also have lease payments to make, so it is actually a liability that no creditor would want to assume.

Drawbacks of Equity Stripping

As with anything, there are a few drawbacks to this strategy.

First, it's complex, usually requiring the help of a sophisticated attorney to structure, draft, and maintain documents. Moreover, managing the liens and the relationships between the entities can add complexity to one's financial situation.

Second, implementing equity stripping after a lawsuit has been initiated or when one is imminent can be deemed a fraudulent transfer or fraudulent conveyance. This means the courts can reverse the transaction. Remember, the time to fix the roof is when the sun is shining, not while it's raining.

Third, it's essential that any lien, mortgage, or lease be legitimate. There should be actual consideration and loan documentation. If it's merely a sham, a court might set it aside.

And don't forget potential tax implications, especially since interest should be charged on the loan, which is an income to one entity and an expense to another.

In sum, not everyone needs a winter coat. But if you're in a blizzard, it may be wise to consult a sophisticated asset protection attorney to help you determine and navigate making your coat.

9

LEGAL STRATEGIES
TO AVOID

We've talked about some great legal strategies that everyone should consider. But there are also some strategies that are often recommended by so-called experts that, in my opinion, are bad ideas and should be avoided at all costs. In this chapter, we'll explore some of the more popular legal strategies that I'd definitely avoid.

Avoid Putting Your House into an LLC

It may be tempting to place your personal residence into an LLC to protect the equity in your home, which, for many, is their largest asset. There are two main problems with this legal strategy.

First, if you're a homeowner, you know that you get several tax benefits from homeownership, the two biggest of which are the mortgage interest deduction and the capital gains exclusion. Currently, if you're single when you sell your home, the first $250,000 in capital gain is excluded from capital gains taxes. If you're married, that amount goes up to $500,000. These are significant tax savings.

Now, if you decide to transfer your home into an LLC for asset protection purposes, you need to do it properly. This would entail not only transferring the title of the property from your personal name into the name of the LLC, but also entering into a rental agreement with your LLC. This means you'd pay rent to your LLC and the LLC would then pay the mortgage. All expenses associated with the home would be paid by the LLC, just like they would if you were the landlord of a rental property.

Of course, when this happens, you may lose your beloved tax benefits because you're no longer a homeowner, but rather a renter. And the LLC may not have access to the capital gains exclusion.

To be fair, this is not a settled issue. If you were to ask three CPAs whether any of these tax advantages are lost when transferring into an LLC, you're likely to get five different answers. Although simply transferring your home into the LLC may not affect the tax classification, the additional steps needed to turn this into a legitimate business operation for asset protection purposes may complicate your tax situation. Given that there's a better way to protect the equity in your home without jeopardizing your tax status (see below), this strategy should be avoided.

 WARNING

Your tax benefits may be at risk, so check with your tax adviser before transferring your personal residence into an LLC. Moving your home into an LLC might jeopardize those valuable tax breaks.

The second issue is that most people who attempt this strategy simply create an LLC in the state where they reside and where the property is located. If you happen to live in a state that has poor asset protection laws, such as California, simply placing the home into a California LLC may not provide you with the level of protection that you envisioned. Worse yet, you have a false sense of security and thus don't explore other options that may actually work—such as equity stripping your house, as discussed in the previous chapter.

The Triad

The example above with your home is a good reminder to talk a little bit about the Triad. The Triad is a concept that my good friend Robert Helms introduced me to. In general, most people are concerned with three things when it comes to structuring their investments: saving on taxes, asset protection, and privacy (see Figure 9.1).

Fig. 9.1

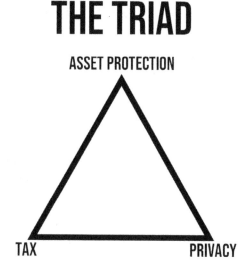

THE TRIAD
ASSET PROTECTION
TAX   PRIVACY

Unfortunately, in some instances, it's impossible to have all three. If saving on taxes is the most important thing for you right now, you may need to give up privacy or asset protection to maximize tax benefits. Conversely, if privacy has become of the utmost importance, maybe your asset protection will be compromised. Above is a classic example with your home in which asset protection and taxes may not mix. Another example is investments in many oil and gas structures. To get the great tax benefits, you often need to be part of a general partnership in which you have unlimited exposure. It's that exposure that grants you the tax benefit.

Avoid Using an S Corporation

First, from an asset protection standpoint, there's no separate legal entity called an S corporation. But there are corporations that can make what's called an *S election* under Subchapter S of one of the IRS chapters. These special types of corporations are generally referred to as "S Corporations" or "S Corps." This allows shareholders of corporations the same pass-through tax treatment as partnerships, meaning shareholders are taxed at the individual level only, on their personal tax returns. Without such an election, the corporation would first get taxed at the corporate level (currently 21 percent for federal, plus each state's corporate tax rate). Then, after dividends are distributed to the shareholders, the owners of the corporations would also get taxed on those dividends on their individual tax returns. Essentially, without the S election, corporate profits are double taxed.

For example, if a corporation has $100 profit, $21 of that would first be taken for federal taxes. This would leave $79 in profit. When you took that profit as a distribution (known as a dividend), you'd also get taxed on that at your personal tax rate. Let's assume your personal tax rate is 25 percent. An additional $19.75 would be taken in taxes, for a total of $40.75 in taxes.

That's more than 40 percent! And that's only at the federal level. You then have to calculate the state corporate tax rate and personal tax rate. With an S election, the entire $100 simply passes to your personal tax return, and thus only $25 would be paid at the federal tax level.

What you may not know is that the S election isn't something unique to corporations. You can make S elections on LLCs and LPs as well. This is what makes LLCs, for example, such a popular entity structure. They have ultimate flexibility on how they get taxed. They can be completely disregarded for tax purposes if taxed as a single member, as a partnership, with an S election, or as a regular C corporation.

So if your CPA advises you that the best tax treatment for your entity is an S Corp, just realize that you can create a regular corporation and make an S election, or you can set up an LLC and make the exact same S election.

Which brings us to the legal strategy angle of S corporations. Unlike LLCs, shareholders of corporations (whether taxed as a regular C corporation or an S corporation) don't benefit from charging order protection. Remember Bob, who injured Skateboarder Sam? Well, if Bob owned a corporation that was taxed as an S corporation, he wouldn't have any protection against a personal judgment against him. His shares in that S corporation would have the same protection as his Apple stock, Google stock, or any other stock he owned in his brokerage account. In other words, *no* protection. The judge can simply order Bob to turn over his shares in the corporation to Skateboarder Sam until his judgment is satisfied.

So, if your tax adviser recommends that you tax your entity as an S corporation, take their advice. But I recommend you set up an LLC, then have it elected to be taxed as an S corporation. That way, you'd have both the asset protection and the tax benefits outlined by your tax professional.

PRO TIP

There's only one state in the entire nation that extends charging order protection to shareholders in a corporation. Not surprisingly, it's Nevada. So, if you're already stuck with a corporation and want to change to an LLC, you won't be able to simply transfer all the assets into a new LLC because this will likely have adverse tax consequences. Instead, look to move your corporation from your current state to Nevada. This is called a redomicile.

So then why would you ever create an actual corporation? In some advanced scenarios, the benefits of the corporation may outweigh the asset protection element. For example, if you intend to take your company public, most experts agree that a corporate structure is preferable. And if you intend to offer stock options to your employees or vendors, a corporate structure will be much more straightforward.

Avoid Putting Your Car in an LLC

There's no better way to get a false sense of security than by putting your personal vehicle into an LLC and thinking that you have some sort of liability protection.

Why?

Because there are actually two responsible parties anytime you get into a car accident or injure someone with your vehicle. Yes, the owner of the vehicle is legally responsible. But so is the driver. So even if you're successful in avoiding personal liability on the ownership side by placing the title of the vehicle into an LLC, if you're the driver of the vehicle, you're personally responsible anyway.

Ownership in an LLC doesn't automatically avoid liability for the owner LLC either. When you place a personal vehicle into a business entity, yet continue the personal use of it, this mixed use can muddy the legal waters. It can give ammunition to the courts to disregard the LLC because you're not separating your business assets from your personal assets. In other words, you're commingling your business and personal assets, which, as we discussed in Chapter 2, is one of the easiest ways to pierce the corporate veil of your LLC.

And let's not forget insurance. In an LLC, you'll be required to obtain commercial auto insurance, which often comes with higher premiums than personal auto insurance. While commercial policies offer more extensive coverage, it might be overkill for your personal vehicle.

But what if you have driving-age children who live with you and use your vehicle? The LLC won't help you there, either. Again, in most jurisdictions, the owner of the vehicle is responsible for any damages resulting in an injury, regardless of who's driving. Many states also require parents to sign financial responsibility forms when their children obtain their permits and driver's licenses. And there is a myriad of other laws that make parents responsible for their children's actions involving negligent entrustment and parental responsibility laws.

The bottom line is, placing your personal vehicle into an LLC will only give you a false sense of security and complicate your life unnecessarily. Instead of placing your personal vehicle in an LLC, just recognize that this is a personal liability exposure and focus on layering your protection, as we discussed in Chapter 1. First, make sure you max out your current personal auto insurance policy (typically capped at $300,000 per injured person), then add your umbrella policy as your next layer of protection. Finally, ensure that you've removed personal ownership of all your valuable assets, implementing the own nothing, control everything strategy outlined in Chapter 2.

When It's OK to Place Your Vehicle in an LLC

If you truly have a business vehicle that's primarily used for business, it may make sense to place it into an LLC. This is especially true if you have employees in your business who use the vehicle. In this case, if one of your employees were to get into an accident while driving the company vehicle, it's the company that stands legally responsible, not the individual business owner. Thus, only the assets of the business are exposed to any potential litigation or claims. Your personal assets, such as your home, bank accounts, and other valuable possessions, remain shielded from any potential fallout. And with the equity stripping strategies outlined in Chapter 8, you should be able to strip most of your business assets away from the company and place them out of the reach of litigants. Also consider placing the vehicle in its own LLC with adequate insurance and having your business entity own the vehicle LLC, or having the business lease the vehicle from the vehicle LLC.

Avoid Series LLCs

There, I said it! To be fair, if you asked ten asset protection attorneys whether they like series LLCs, you'd likely get about 60 percent against and 40 percent in favor of those structures. A series LLC is a special type of LLC that's only recognized in twenty-two states. These states have written into their statutes that LLCs set up in their state can create separate *series* or *cells* inside the LLC that have unique characteristics. Each of these series operates like a separate entity with its own assets, members, and liabilities, distinct from the other series and distinct from the main LLC. So if one series incurs a liability, only the assets of that particular series are typically at risk and not the assets of another series or the master LLC. This arrangement can be especially beneficial for businesses managing multiple operations or assets.

In addition, series LLCs provide cost and time savings. Instead of having to create a separate LLC every time you have a new asset to protect, a simple internal document is created (usually taken from a template), and voilà! A new series is created, saving both time and the cost associated with filing for a separate LLC.

However, while the concept is appealing, it does have its drawbacks. Chief among those drawbacks, I'd say, is the overreliance on them for asset protection. These are relatively new structures and they haven't been tested in court—especially when legal issues arise in different states.

Remember, the majority of states don't recognize the series LLC structure, and there may be uncertainties about how these entities are treated across state lines or in litigation. For example, let's assume a tenant slips and falls in one of your properties in Atlanta, Georgia. The tenant sues the owner of your Georgia property, which happens to be one of your independent cells within your Nevada series LLC. Georgia is one of the states that doesn't recognize series LLCs. So the real risk arises that the Georgia court won't recognize the cell as a separate liability shield and will enter a judgment against the master

LLC, exposing all of the rental properties that the master LLC owns through the other cells.

The American Bar Association has also refused to endorse series LLCs, which I'm sure will be used in any court challenge that will eventually come.

Whether you decide to go with a series LLC or not, it's crucial to consult with legal counsel that's familiar with series LLCs before proceeding with this structure. But, for me, I'd avoid them because I think they provide a false sense of security since we really don't know if they'll hold up in court.

PRO TIP

Here are the twenty-two states that currently recognize series LLCs as of this writing.

1.	Alabama	12.	Nevada
2.	Arkansas	13.	North Dakota
3.	Delaware	14.	Oklahoma
4.	District of Columbia	15.	Ohio
5.	Illinois	16.	South Dakota
6.	Indiana	17.	Tennessee
7.	Iowa	18.	Texas
8.	Kansas	19.	Utah
9.	Minnesota	20.	Virginia
10.	Missouri	21.	Wisconsin
11.	Montana	22.	Wyoming

Avoid Putting Too Many Assets in One Entity

A question that I get all the time is, "Mauricio, how many properties or assets can I put into one LLC? I really don't want to incur the time and expense needed to create a brand-new LLC every time I acquire a new property or asset."

The answer here is different for everyone. The only legal concept you need to understand is that each asset inside your LLC is exposed to the other assets in that LLC. So, for example, say you put three rental properties inside one LLC. If a tenant slips and falls on one of the properties and obtains a judgment against the LLC that owns the property, the judgment creditor will not only be able to access the equity in that property, but also the equity in the other two properties. Plus, whatever cash that LLC has in the bank and any other assets it owns will be fair game for the judgment creditor.

So the real question becomes, how comfortable are you with that scenario? If you have $150,000 in equity in all three properties, but you own $20 million in real estate in total, it's probably not a big deal. But if those three properties are all you own, one injury could be devastating and could wipe you out completely.

So it really has less to do with how many assets are inside one entity, and more to do with what the value of those assets adds up to. In other words, it's about how much equity is inside each LLC. Having said that, you also need to account for the fact that it's usually not practical to have each property in its own LLC due to the administrative costs and time-consuming nature of that strategy. So it really is about striking the right balance for you.

I remember back in 2010, shortly after the financial crisis, I was helping out a client who had fifty single-family rental properties. Around half of them had negative equity, meaning he owed more on those houses than they were worth. Well, for those houses, we decided to put them all in one LLC. If something happened to one of those twenty-five properties, there was nothing for a plaintiff to take if a judgment was obtained against the LLC. We simply insulated the liability against the other houses.

All this is to say focus on the equity or value of the assets in the LLC instead of the number of assets in it.

Avoid Single-Member LLCs When Possible

In Chapter 2, we went over the charging order protection that LLCs and LPs enjoy, which is why entities like those are so powerful. Recall that there's a public policy reason behind extending charging order protection to those businesses. When two or more business partners are working together, our judicial system doesn't want to disrupt their business by allowing a judgment creditor to step into one of the partners' shoes and forcing the other partners to do business with them. After all, the judgment creditor is not interested in continuing to run the business, but rather wants to liquidate the assets of the business to satisfy their judgment.

So to protect this partnership, the law protects the nonjudgment partner by not allowing the judgment creditor to become a partner in the business. Instead, it limits the judgment creditor to whatever distributions the partner would've received from the business.

But when you think about this, the logic used doesn't make sense when you have a single-member LLC. There's no business partner to protect, so the argument doesn't really translate. As a result, there are very few states (five to be exact) that officially extend charging order protection to single-member LLCs. Therefore, as a general strategy, I advise clients to form legitimate multi-member LLCs whenever possible. This way, the odds of obtaining a charging order to protect them increases significantly.

WARNING

When establishing an LLC, ensure that your business partner isn't just a "nominal" or "de minimis" owner, meaning they have a very trivial, negligible, or very minor ownership percentage just to make the LLC a multi-member entity. Make sure your partner contributes real money for their ownership percentage and participates in the operation of the business.

Having a single-member LLC also increases the odds of the corporate veil being pierced, since having no partner increases the risk of not following corporate formalities and the odds of not operating the LLC as a separate entity from its owner. This might happen when the single-member LLC commingles personal and business funds, doesn't maintain proper business records, or fails to treat the LLC as a separate entity. This is less likely to occur when one has a business partner.

10

RAPID-FIRE LEGAL STRATEGIES

Throughout this book, I've outlined the legal strategies that I believe are the most important strategies to consider. But there are other strategies out there that didn't quite warrant their own chapter since they're fairly straightforward. So in this chapter, we finish with a rapid-fire section of several additional strategies to keep in mind.

Keep Great Records

Keeping great records helps you not only to stay organized, but could be the difference between keeping and losing your assets, winning or losing a lawsuit, and saving you thousands if not hundreds of thousands of dollars in legal fees. Keeping great records, however, assumes you created great documents in the first place, so let's start there.

One of the best ways to save money by avoiding conflicts in the future is to have your legal documents properly drafted by a professional. When you prepare legal documents on your own, whether they be independent contracts with vendors, employment agreements with your employees, or operating agreements with your business partners, these documents can leave you exposed. They may be fine initially to get into the relationship and may even be fine to refer back to once in a while to see what some basic parameters were. But if there's ever a legal dispute, or you want to initiate a claim because you feel you were wronged, do you think your do-it-yourself or template agreement will be a good document to rely on in court? How likely do you think it will be that an opposing attorney will find holes in your agreements?

It amazes me how many people draft their own legal contracts to save money up front. Instead, they should be using a professional who truly understands their particular set of circumstances and knows which questions to ask to craft an agreement that covers all the possible outcomes of the relationship.

WARNING

DIY documents? Think twice! Do-it-yourself legal documents might seem cost-effective in the short run, but they can end up costing you much more in legal fees and stress if they're challenged in court. Investing in a professional contract attorney up front can save you from a myriad of potential legal issues down the road.

I can't stress enough the importance of having a basic contract attorney on speed dial. Someone who you can ask to prepare your minor contracts, such as independent contractor agreements for vendors, employment letters/contracts, operating agreements, or nondisclosure and noncompete agreements. Will it cost you more up front? Of course. A litigation attorney, however, is exponentially more expensive in the long run than a great contract attorney.

Second, from an asset protection standpoint, you'll want to have a solid corporate records book, which, admittedly these days, is more apt to be a digital folder on your hard drive. You want to make sure you're following all the corporate formalities that your formation attorney has recommended and save all the documents in the folder specific to your LLC. You'll want this binder or folder to contain the basic formation documents, operating agreements, and employment identification number. You'll also want to make sure your meeting minutes, corporate resolutions, financials, and tax returns are all there.

 PRO TIP

Though we often refer to "corporate records books," in today's digital age it's more common to maintain these records digitally. Just ensure they're backed up securely and accessible when needed.

Legal publisher Nolo has a great reference called *The Corporate Records Handbook,* which I highly recommend and is the one I have on my shelf. At the end of the day, if an attorney sends you a legal document request asking for your entity binder, you don't want to send over just three measly documents. You want to send them the most robust set of documents that show off how you've been treating your company seriously and as a separate corporate entity, legally separate and distinct from you.

You may also want to periodically keep track of the contracts you already have in place to make sure they're up to date. Is your will current? Does your will account for the major life events that have transpired since you drafted them, such as more children, caring for your elderly parents, or adding family pets to your household? Have your LLC operating agreements been reviewed and kept pace with the ever-changing business? Have you been preparing amendments to your operating agreements when partners are added, managers change, additional rules have been outlined for your business? Are your insurance policies up to date?

Finally, remember to document your phone conversations with vendors and people you do business with, so you have appropriate records if you find yourself in a future dispute. I recommend following up most phone conversations with an e-mail confirming the content of the conversation. Something along the lines of, "This e-mail will confirm our telephone conversation of last Monday in which we discussed X, Y, and Z." It helps support your version of the facts and avoids the "he said, she said" dilemma, which you'll have the burden to prove if you're looking to start a claim.

All of these little things add up to ensuring that, in the event of any dispute, you can easily access documents and be confident that they're as airtight as possible. This way, you can properly defend yourself against any allegation or initiate a claim against someone who has violated the terms of your agreement.

Consider Prenuptial and Postnuptial Agreements

Putting aside the religious aspects of it, marriage is a legal contract between two people, governed by the laws of the state in which they reside. Similar to wills, discussed in Chapter 3, the marriage contract is typically outlined in each state statute. States are generally split between "community property" states, where all assets accumulated during marriage are split evenly in the event of a divorce; and "equitable distribution" states, where assets accumulated during marriage are split in a "fair" manner in the event of a divorce.

Determining Fair and Equitable Distributions

Fair and equitable distribution in divorce refers to the fair and just division of marital assets and liabilities based on various factors, rather than a strict equal split. While many believe that a fifty-fifty division is standard, this isn't always the most equitable solution. For instance, one spouse may have brought significant student debt into the marriage, which they alone benefited from; in such cases, courts might decide that this debt shouldn't be equally shared.

Factors that courts consider in determining an equitable division include the age and health of the spouses. An older spouse or one with poor health might receive more assets due to reduced earning potential. The total assets and debts each spouse bring into the marriage, as well as those accrued during the marriage, are also considered.

Earning power, potential tax implications of asset division, and each spouse's individual income also play roles in the division process. A spouse with a higher earning potential might receive fewer assets, given their capability to rebuild financial stability. The length of the marriage can also influence decisions; longer marriages may see more balanced splits due to intertwined finances. In sum, equitable contribution seeks a balance that recognizes individual contributions, needs, and circumstances in a divorce.

....

This is where prenuptial agreements, often referred to as "prenups," and postnuptial agreements come into play. They replace the agreement that the government has outlined for you in their divorce statutes. Some states have certain limits on what you can change, especially when it comes to child support. But these agreements generally lay out the ownership of their respective assets and stipulate how those assets will be divided in the event of a divorce, separation, or death. A postnuptial agreement is essentially the same as a prenup, but is entered into after the marriage as opposed to before the marriage.

Both agreements bring clarity and can prevent potential disputes in the future, so it's a strategy worth exploring. Although, I must admit, it's a difficult discussion to have right before you get married. But by outlining who owns what from the outset, or deciding on the distribution of assets acquired during the marriage, couples can ensure a fair distribution based on mutual understanding, rather than leaving it to the potentially tumultuous and emotionally charged environment of divorce proceedings.

At its core, prenuptial and postnuptial agreements are asset protection strategies that focus on your future or current spouse, rather than a judgment creditor. They can also address debts. For example, if one spouse has significant debt coming into the marriage, a prenuptial agreement can ensure that the other spouse is protected from those debts. Unfortunately, some states allow non-debtor spouses to be on the hook for the debts incurred by the debtor spouse.

Equity Strip Your Home

Placing your personal residence in an LLC doesn't really work to protect the equity in your home, as we discussed in the previous chapter. The best way to protect your home equity is to strip it away and put it in another safe place—ideally, in an LLC in a top asset protection state and owned by an APT. Obtaining a third-party loan secured by the equity in your home, however, is probably the cleanest way to do this. A bank or third-party lender loans your LLC money. In exchange, the lender gets a promissory note and records a second (or first) lien on your home, which wipes out the equity. This can be a traditional loan or a HELOC. By obtaining a loan through your LLC, you essentially move the equity from a dangerous place (your home) into a safe place (your protected LLC).

So when an attorney does an asset search on you prior to taking on a client to potentially sue you, they'll find your home, but with little or no equity in the house because of the loans. Thus, there's nothing for the attorney to go after. Even if you're in the middle of a lawsuit and a judgment is obtained against you, the original mortgage on your house—plus the second lien—would need to be paid off in a foreclosure before anyone would see any money. Therefore, judgment creditors are unlikely to foreclose on your home.

But what if you don't want to or can't get a third-party loan?

A common equity stripping strategy is to become your own bank and use your own LLC to act as the lender to place a friendly lien on your property. The exact same process should be followed as described above. The LLC makes a loan or provides a line of credit to you at a reasonable interest rate, then places a second (or first) lien on your home to secure the loan. Ideally, the entire loan is made and transferred from one bank account to another to evidence the loan.

But, even if you can't make the entire loan, a line of credit will require a mortgage for the full amount.

 WARNING

Only the actual money lent out will protect the equity. So if you don't lend the entire amount up front, make sure you constantly draw from your line of credit over the years to eventually withdraw the entire amount. But even if it's only a line of credit, the second mortgage will still show up on the attorney's search and thus be a major disincentive for the attorney to consider your home as a potential target.

Have a White-Collar Criminal Defense Attorney on Speed Dial

We didn't really discuss any criminal legal strategies, primarily because I'm a practicing civil attorney and I'm unqualified to speak about those. However, one strategy I can definitely recommend is ensuring that you research and find a good criminal defense attorney to have on speed dial.

You want to be in a position in which, if something terrible happens to you and you find yourself in the back seat of a police car, you and your spouse have somebody in your phone who you can call without hesitation. This isn't the time to start thinking about which lawyer you can call and having your spouse or family research someone who can represent you and visit you in jail. You want to be prepared.

This is especially true if you own firearms, even if you have them only in your home for self-defense. But other unexpected criminal issues can arise, such as serious car accidents in which someone is killed, or unexpected fights in which someone is seriously injured.

Last, but certainly not least, knowing that expert legal counsel is just a phone call away offers peace of mind and the knowledge that you're well prepared for potential criminal challenges.

If you found yourself in the back seat of a police car this evening, who would *you* call?

WARNING

Prepare for unexpected legal challenges: even if you lead a law-abiding life, unforeseen incidents can happen that may have you answering to the legal authorities. Having a reputable criminal defense attorney's contact information saved in your phone can provide peace of mind.

Sufficiently Capitalize Your LLCs

We've spent quite some time exploring all the benefits of owning businesses and holding assets in an LLC to provide you with protection from your assets. However, no matter how great your LLC structures are, if your LLCs aren't adequately capitalized, you risk the possibility of a judge "piercing the corporate veil," allowing a judgment creditor to reach your personal assets. *Capitalizing* an LLC refers to the process of funding or providing financial resources to the LLC, often in the form of equity or debt.

Piercing the corporate veil usually happens when the LLC is viewed as an "alter ego" of its owner, rather than a separate entity. Sufficient capitalization is evidence that you've made a genuine investment and commitment to your company. Always remember that if your LLC faces a lawsuit, one strategy attorney's employ is to claim that the company was undercapitalized, making it a mere shell or facade. This claim can be a precursor to an attempt to pierce the corporate veil. Having a record of adequate capitalization can counteract such strategies from the outset.

One of the easiest ways to accomplish this is to have an insurance policy that's expected to handle reasonable claims based on the type of activity your LLC conducts. Having reasonable start-up capital in the company also helps, because it shows that you have something to lose.

Whether or not you implement any of the legal strategies in this chapter, or any of the other legal strategies mentioned throughout this book, I hope that I've at least opened your eyes to all the options that are out there and are available to you if and when you need them. I encourage you to return to this book every now and then as you continue on your life's journey. Some strategies may not be relevant today, but may become beneficial in the future.

If you have any questions about anything in this book, I encourage you to reach out to me and simply ask, at www.AskMauricio .com. I look forward to hearing from you.

GLOSSARY

addendums: additions to a completed insurance policy that add, delete, exclude, or change insurance coverage. In the context of insurance, addendums are synonymous with riders.

balance transfers: Some credit cards provide you with checks so you can write a check to yourself or directly to another bank or credit card to pay off outstanding loans. This allows you to transfer balances from one credit card to another. There is no requirement on how to use the funds from the check, so you can use them to invest or for any other purpose.

blockchain: a distributed database that maintains a continuously growing list of ordered records, called "blocks." These blocks are linked using cryptography. Each block contains a cryptographic hash of the previous block, a time stamp, and transaction data. A blockchain is a decentralized, distributed, and public digital ledger that is used to record transactions across many computers so that the record cannot be altered retroactively without the alteration of all subsequent blocks and the consensus of the network.

corporate veil: refers to the legal concept that separates the actions and liabilities of a corporation (or limited liability company, LLC) from its shareholders, owners, or members. When a business is properly incorporated, it is treated as a separate legal entity distinct from the individuals who own or operate it.

decentralized: refers to the distribution and delegation of power, authority, and responsibility away from a central location or governing body. In a decentralized system, control is spread across multiple locations or among various individuals or entities. This contrasts with centralized systems, where a single central authority has a concentration of control.

defendant: the party who is sued by a plaintiff in court.

depositions: the process of interviewing a witness or party to a lawsuit under oath before a court reporter in a place away from the courtroom before the trial. The interview (known as testimony) is taken down by the court reporter, who will prepare a transcript that assists in trial preparation.

discovery: the process during a lawsuit in which the parties to the lawsuit exchange information and documentation relating to the lawsuit in preparation for the trial.

encumber: to burden an asset (in our context, usually a piece of real estate) with a claim or legal liability, such as a mortgage or a lien, that may restrict the owner's ability to use or dispose of the asset freely. Encumbrances can affect the transferability of the asset and can also reduce its value.

equity: the resulting value of an asset after deducting all the liabilities owed by that asset.

Fannie Mae: the Federal National Mortgage Association (FNMA), commonly known as "Fannie Mae."

fiduciary: a person or organization that acts on behalf of another person or persons, putting their clients' interest ahead of their own, with a duty to reserve good faith and trust. Being a fiduciary requires being bound both legally and ethically to act in the other's best interests.

Freddie Mac: the Federal Home Loan Mortgage Corporation (FHLMC), commonly known as "Freddie Mac."

frivolous lawsuit: a lawsuit that's filed with no substantial basis in law or fact, and little to no chance of being won.

gross value: the total value of something before any deductions, such as expenses, taxes, or discounts are applied.

irrevocable: unchangeable. In the context of trusts, an irrevocable trust is one that can't be changed once created. This compares to a *revocable* trust that can be changed.

judgment creditor: the winning plaintiff in a lawsuit, to whom the court decides the defendant owes money.

judgment debtor: the losing defendant in a lawsuit, whom the court decides owes money to the plaintiff.

litigious: involved in a lot of lawsuits.

net value: the total value of something after all deductions, such as expenses, taxes, or discounts are applied.

plaintiff: the party that is initiating a lawsuit by filing a complaint in court.

proof of concept: a demonstration with the primary goal of verifying that certain concepts or theories have the potential for real-world application.

revocable: capable of being canceled, taken back, or changed. In the context of trusts, a revocable trust is a trust that can be changed or amended at a future date. This compares to an *irrevocable* trust that cannot be changed.

riders: additions to a completed insurance policy that add, delete, exclude, or change insurance coverage. In the context of insurance, this is an addition to your regular insurance policy that adds specific coverage. Riders are synonymous with addendums.

spendthrift: in the context of a trust, a clause that prevents beneficiaries from pledging, selling, or assigning their expected trust distributions to others.

stock dividends: the profit that owners of corporations receive when the corporation decides to distribute profits.

stock options: a contract that gives you the right, but not the obligation, to purchase a stock at a predetermined price.

substantive relationship: a relationship that's formed when the person offering an investment has sufficient information to evaluate whether a potential investor has sufficient knowledge and expertise in financial and business matters to be able to evaluate the merits and risks of a particular investment.

surrender: refers to the insurance policyholder's decision to cancel their life insurance policy before the maturity date or insured event occurs.

tenants-in-common: a way to hold title to property in which two or more people have an *undivided interest* (see definition below) in the property and all have equal rights to use the property, even if the percentages of ownership aren't equal.

undivided interest: title to real property held by two or more persons without specifying the interests of each party by percentage or description of a portion of the real estate. Such interests are typical between tenants-in-common.

ENDNOTES

1   One Legal. "Top court filing statistics from around the country." https://www.onelegal.com/blog/top-court-filing-statistics-from-around-the-country/#:~:text=It%27s%20estimated%20that%20there%20are,registered%20lawyers%20exceed%20one%20million.

2   World Population Review. "Lawyers Per Capita by Country 2023." https://worldpopulationreview.com/country-rankings/lawyers-per-capita-by-country#:~:text=United%20States&text=There%20are%20more%20lawyers%20per,California%20and%20Florida%20close%20behind.

3   The Babcock Law Firm LLC. "Frivolous Lawsuits: What Are They and How Do They Affect You?" https://www.injurylawcolorado.com/tort-law/frivolous-lawsuits/.

4   E.R. Munro and Company. "Your Chances of Getting Sued." https://ermunro.com/blog/your-chances-of-getting-sued/#:~:text=Americans%20have%20a%2010%20percent,%2C%20an%20international%20investment%20firm.

5   O'Reilly, Kevin B. "1 in 3 physicians has been sued; by age 55, 1 in 2 hit with suit." (American Medical Association, 2018). https://www.ama-assn.org/practice-management/sustainability/1-3-physicians-has-been-sued-age-55-1-2-hit-suit.

6   Fontinelle, Amy. "What Exactly Can Be Taken From You In a Lawsuit?" *Forbes Advisor*, 2023. https://www.forbes.com/advisor/homeowners-insurance/what-can-be-taken-in-lawsuit/#:~:text="The%20situations%20where%20lawsuits%20cause,"%20said%20Edward%20Y.%20Lee%2C.

7   A 2021 Gallup poll found that only forty-six percent of American adults have a will. This suggests that more than half of all American adults don't have a will in place. https://news.gallup.com/poll/351500/how-many-americans-have-will.aspx.

8   American Bar Association. "Directory of Law School Public Interest & Pro Bono Programs." https://www.americanbar.org/groups/center-pro-bono/resources/directory_of_law_school_public_interest_pro_bono_programs/.

9   O'Connell, Ann. "50-State Chart of Small Claims Court Dollar Limits." Nolo.com. https://www.nolo.com/legal-encyclopedia/small-claims-suits-how-much-30031.html.

10 Everplans. "State-by-State Digital Estate Planning Laws." https://www.everplans.com/articles/state-by-state-digital-estate-planning-laws.

ACKNOWLEDGMENTS

Writing this book has been an incredible journey, one that I could not have embarked on without the support and expertise of many remarkable individuals.

To my wife, Heidi, and my two little angels, Adelina and Alessandra, who I have dedicated this book to: You are my why. To my parents, Hugo and Monica, for your love, encouragement, and the countless ways you've supported me throughout my life. This book owes much to your unwavering belief in me. To Ken McElroy, for believing in me and providing me this opportunity to write my first full-blown book. I cherish our friendship more than you know. To Marla Markman, my incredible project manager: Thank you for putting up with this rookie author, and for your patience, commitment, and guidance. To my amazing editors, Erin Brenner and Wendy Scavuzzo: Thanks for taking my average writing abilities and making me look like a pro. My heartfelt thanks for your exceptional editing skills. To the amazing and incomparable, Jennifer Costanza: What would I have done without you? Thanks for putting up with my random and late-night texts and always being there every step of the way. And finally, to by law partner, Bethanty LaFlam and the rest of the Premier Law Group team: Thank you for giving me the space and understanding needed to pursue this endeavor. Your support has been a gift I deeply appreciate.

Each of you has played a significant role in this journey, and I am immensely grateful for your contributions. Thank you for being part of this story.

INDEX

ABOUT THE AUTHOR

Known as "one of the few lawyers who actually speaks English," Mauricio J. Rauld helps real estate syndicators stay out of jail by ensuring full compliance with federal and state securities laws. With more than twenty-four years of legal experience, Mauricio is one of the premier real estate syndication attorneys in the country.

Mauricio was recently featured on the cover of the *Top 100* magazine as a Top 100 Attorney and has previously been recognized as one of the top California attorneys under forty by *Super Lawyers* magazine.

As an educator at heart, Mauricio is the legal adviser for Ken McElroy (Rich Dad Advisor with more than $2 billion in real estate acquisitions) and has recorded several videos on legal strategies for real estate investors on Ken's YouTube channel. He also hosts his own legal YouTube channel and is the host of two popular podcasts: *Real Estate Syndicator LIVE* and *Drunk Real Estate*. He regularly travels around the country speaking to real estate investors.

A graduate of the University of California at Berkeley, Mauricio lives in Southern California with his wife, Heidi, and their little angels, Adelina and Alessandra.

PREMIER
LAW GROUP

Your Premier Syndication Attorneys

For FREE real estate syndication guides
for both GPs and passive investors, sign up at
www.premierlawgroup.net.

You will gain access to popular ebooks, like *5 Things Every Syndicator Must Know to Stay Out of Jail* and *Top 10 Questions to Ask Any Deal Sponsor Before Investing in a Private Syndication.*

You will also receive Mauricio's popular "Mondays with Mauricio" weekly email series where thousands of GPs and LPs get cutting-edge insights into syndication and asset protection strategies.

Plus, you will gain access to Mauricio's checklist on how to become an accredited investor without having to satisfy any income or net worth requirements. It is invaluable for BOTH passive investors trying to find incredible real estate deals and syndicators who can get more of their investor base if they become accredited.

THE TOP 100 ATTORNEYS

Mauricio J. Rauld, Esq., Syndication Attorney

Not only that, but you can also sign up for Mauricio's weekly coaching sessions where he will answer your questions on anything legal.